VOLUME 2

CASH FLOW

Note Brokering

Library of Congress in Publication Data
October 04
Txu-1-204-543

Cash Flow Note Broker

10 9 8 7 6 5 4 3 2 1

The enclosed material is designed for educational purposes only. Each State may have different certification and specific guidelines. Please refer to your State for additional and future information. The information contained herein is considered correct at the time of creation but laws and regulations are updated frequently and the reader assumes the responsibility for confirming current regulations and applicable data. The publisher and author make no warranty as to the success of the individuals using the training material contained herein. The publisher and author make no warranty as to any action taken by any individual completing this program. The reader is responsible for the appropriate use of the materials and information provided.

This publication is designed to provide accurate and authoritative information concerning the subject matter. All material is sold with the understanding that neither the author nor the publisher guarantees the actions of any individual making use of the inclusions. Neither the author nor the publisher is rendering a legal opinion, accounting recommendation or other professional service. If legal advice or other expert assistance is desired, the services of a legal professional or other individual should be sought.

The applicable federally released forms, disclosures and notices are generated from public domain. Copyright law does apply to all intellectual materials and all rights under said law are reserved b y the copyright owner.

Coursework is available at special quantity discounts to use as premiums and sales promotions within corporate or private training programs. To obtain information or inquire about availability please write to Director, PO Box 1, Hollidaysburg, PA 16648.

CASH FLOW

Note Brokering

Congratulations on your decision to enter the exciting field of Note Brokering. Few other opportunities provide the potential for success, career stability and incredible profits that you will find in the field of Note Brokering. The field of Note Brokering contains numerous opportunities for growth, increased income and enhanced job security. Note Brokering is a little understood career field that provides an incredible opportunity to any individual willing to put forth the effort to understand the intricate concepts and activities necessary to achieve success.

Over the coming weeks you will gain the knowledge and tools, you need to capitalize on the unlimited opportunities available to you through the brokering of the various notes that exist in the market but are currently not being sourced by other Note Brokers within your region.

The design of this coursework will provide you with the building blocks you will use to create the solid foundation necessary to begin building your new business. You will obtain the knowledge will require to implement the techniques and strategies necessary to make your note brokering career successful.

You have purchased one of the most powerful and comprehensive courses available on the market. The tools and knowledge incorporated throughout the program will enable you to use the opportunity available within the arena of cash flow notes as the primary tool to grow you income, obtain career stability and become one of the most respected professionals within your community!

Note Brokering provides you with the career option that will make you one of the most highly respected professionals within your community.

You may choose to conduct your business from

> Your home

> In an office

> Within a bank

➢ You will receive an income that relates directly to how hard (or smart) you work.

The pay structure within the note industry is based primarily upon the negotiations you complete in the brokering process. You will be paid based upon the note value, including face amount and interest, note discount that you negotiate and most of all your ability to meet the needs of each party within the process and you get to retain the surplus cash in the transaction. Surplus cash left after the needs of all of the parties to the transaction have been met is your cash!

➢ A Note Broker's business is built around a core customer base of satisfied note sellers.

Each time you create the perfect note package for a seller, oversee a perfect negotiation process and ensure a smooth closing meeting, you grow your business. The note sellers that you work with today will be the referral sources upon which you will build your business. Regardless of where you go within the industry, your exceptional customer service will ensure that your referrals will go with you.

➢ You will have the opportunity to use your creativity and ingenuity to become the best in your chosen profession.

The note process is a series of complicated calculations and delicate negotiations. As a professionally trained note broker, you will be able to overcome all potential roadblocks and smoothly negotiate the transaction so that all individuals who take part in a broker completed by you walk away not only satisfied, but impressed with the process and with your performance!

Through the application of creative thinking and a comprehensive understanding of the note venue, you can blend the needs of the note investor with the desires of the note seller to create the perfect note package for every transaction!

Research has shown that the most important attribute of a successful Note Broker is the drive to succeed within their chosen profession. The drive to succeed surpasses educational degrees, experience and personal attributes within the field of mortgage lending. Purchasing this program shows that you have initial drive needed to begin on the path toward career stability and success and attain top-producer status.

This program will assist you in gaining the base foundation you need to begin your career and allow you to understand and implement the advanced practices you need to become the best within your chosen profession.

Note Brokering is perhaps one of the most satisfying career opportunities available. You will perform a well-paid service that benefits every individual involved in the transaction.

- You will learn all of the industry specific concepts upon which you will build your success

- You will obtain all of the information you will need to understand each facet of the Note Brokering process

- You will master the intricate activities that lead to the achievement of your goals

- You will be able to explain the benefits of note transfer to each party in the transaction

- You will gain the needed skills to plan and implement a marketing strategy that will enable you to locate marketable notes

- You will learn the skills necessary to negotiate the transfer of those notes to build career success

Each segment of the course incorporates essential industry information in a high-impact, easy to understand format that will aid you in becoming the best of your new profession.

Congratulations on your decision to take the first step in gaining career independence. Obtaining a comprehensive understanding of the knowledge necessary in your new career and developing the advanced skills that will lead you to success is the first step to creating the business of your dreams!

Chapter

1

THE POTENTIAL IN NOTE BROKERING

The first step to building a successful Note Brokering business is to gain a comprehensive understanding of the industry and the steps of the brokering process. Note Brokering has grown in popularity in recent years as the return that can be achieved through the purchase of discounted notes becomes more attractive to investors as well as to the seller accepting monthly payments in lieu of a cash settlement. You must gain a comprehensive understanding of the needs of each party to the transaction, the best practices for obtaining, screening and remitting notes and of the place that you can take within this exciting and lucrative field!

Notes exist in every community across America. The ability to locate and source notes is one that is relatively simple to gain. You must gain the fundamental knowledge of where these notes can be located and why they exist. Upon obtaining this fundamental knowledge, you will use your creativity, industry specific knowledge and negotiation skills to bring together the note seller and the note investor in a transaction that is custom-designed to meet the needs of each party.

- When an individual must sell an item of personal or real property, they sometimes find that the sale occurs more quickly if they, as the seller, act as the holder of the note.

- Businesses must frequently accept revolving credit payments from individuals making purchases from the business. These net invoices can easily reach 30, 60, even 90 days.

- When interest rates climb and the real estate market slows, the competition for each buyer becomes fierce. Sellers are sometimes faced with the choice of dramatically reducing the sales price of their property in an effort to sell or waiting an extended period to obtain a suitable offer from a buyer.

  Another option does exist and more sellers are taking advantage of this opportunity than ever before.

  Sellers have the opportunity to sell their home today, for the full value, by holding the note on the sale.

Each of these situations, among others, creates an environment in which an individual seller holds a valuable asset known as a note. This asset brings monthly or installment payments that provide the holder with positive cash flow.

The Note Brokering process provides the opportunity for that Seller, to obtain a lump sum of cash in hand in exchange for the note.

The Seller will often accept a discount off of the face value of the note in exchange for receiving cash in hand. Because notes are valuable in the terms of cash flow, Investors are willing to provide this lump sum in exchange for the immediate equity generated by the discounted figure the original Seller is willing to accept.

Another method that provides the Investor with a profit building opportunity is the interest accumulation. Nearly every note contains an allowance for the payment of interest on the principal balance owed. By purchasing the note, the Investor gains the potential to collect these interest payments. These payments can substantially increase the return the Investor receives on their funds. We will review the benefits of interest payments later in the course. For now, you must simply be aware that notes exist in many forms, in every location and both the Investor and the Seller can benefit from the transaction you will learn to negotiate.

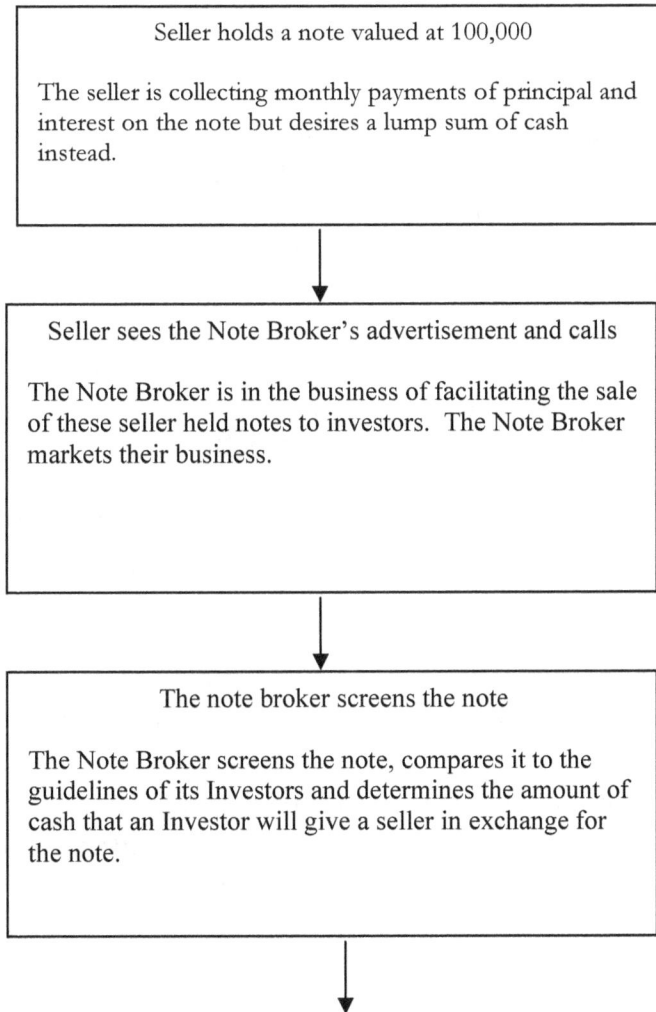

Seller holds a note valued at 100,000

The seller is collecting monthly payments of principal and interest on the note but desires a lump sum of cash instead.

Seller sees the Note Broker's advertisement and calls

The Note Broker is in the business of facilitating the sale of these seller held notes to investors. The Note Broker markets their business.

The note broker screens the note

The Note Broker screens the note, compares it to the guidelines of its Investors and determines the amount of cash that an Investor will give a seller in exchange for the note.

```
┌─────────────────────────────────────────────┐
│            Seller accepts the offer           │
│                                               │
│  The Note Broker will detail the discounted   │
│  offer, in this instance $84,000 that the     │
│  investor will pay the seller today!  The     │
│  seller accepts this discount off the face    │
│  value of their note in exchange for          │
│  receiving cash.                              │
│                                               │
└─────────────────────────────────────────────┘
                        │
                        ▼
┌─────────────────────────────────────────────┐
│               The transfer closes             │
│                                               │
│  The Investor provides the money.             │
│  The Seller obtains the cash payment.         │
│  The Note Broker gets the commission and      │
│  moves on to source the next note.            │
│                                               │
└─────────────────────────────────────────────┘
```

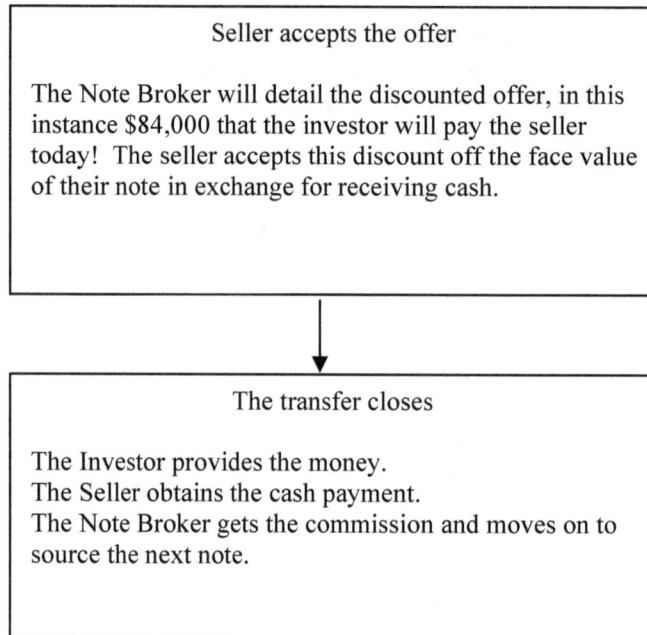

Figure 1:1 – Note Process Overview

You will serve a vital purpose in the note transfer process. You will act as an educator, a negotiator and an advocate for every party in the transaction.

- It is often difficult for a Seller to understand the processes behind note investments. The time and effort necessary to learn note investment basics, locate a potential Investor and negotiate a viable sale are typically more than the average Seller will be willing or able to do.

- Most Investors purchase many, many notes over the term of their investment career. Locating a Seller who may wish to sell, educating the Seller regarding the processes behind note investment, negotiating the purchase and finalizing the transaction would take more time then your average Investor is able to expend on a single transaction.

    Your goal as a Note Broker will be to perform these tasks on behalf of each party.

    ➤ You will be working for the benefit of both the Seller and the Investor

    ➤ You primary goal will be to bring the goals of these two individuals together and assist in negotiating a mutually beneficial transaction for all of the parties involved.

> ➤ You will be able to obtain income for your services through a variety of methods that will be addressed in more detail in the Chapter Negotiating a Commission.
>
> Your function will not just be to locate and bring together these individuals.

> ➤ You must become an educator of the Seller.

> ➤ You must learn to ensure the Investor's funds are well protected.

> ➤ You must become a master negotiator ensuring both parties obtain the negotiation points that are most vital to their situation.

> ➤ Your goal must be the outstanding service you provide to each party with whom you work.

> ➤ You must strive to gain a reputation as a well-trained professional who truly understands every facet of your industry and who negotiates fair, solid transactions that benefit each party.

By ensuring that your actions are impeccable, you will discover that you quickly gain a reputation as the Note Broker who fulfills every promise. This reputation will generate repeat and referral business that will cause your new business to grow and prosper beyond any goal you have set for yourself.

You should structure your business around the premise that every individual involved in the Note Brokering process must walk away from the settlement satisfied that they got the best possible deal available to him or her. The Note Brokering process is in place to allow Investors to obtain the income stream generated from the periodic payments of these notes. The process is in place to allow the seller to obtain the cash in hand that the Investor pays in exchange for the income stream held by the seller.

Your purpose is to act as the negotiation advocate for each party in the transaction. It is up to you to ensure that every party walks away from the settlement feeling that they have achieved their goals.

- The Investor obtains an opportunity to receive a steady income from their investment capital at a high rate of return.

- The Seller obtains a lump sum of cash that they may then use to accomplish their dreams and goals.

- You, as the Note Broker, obtain fair compensation for your efforts in bringing the transaction to close.

Each party benefits through the process in the ways most important to them.

Each individual situation in which you become involved will vary. Any variations from the typical will cause alterations to the flow of the transaction. The following list is an example of a simplified Note Brokering process. You should strive to make your business processes match the sample structure as closely as possible. The sample structure aids in ensuring a smooth flow and minimizing confusion and delays.

The Note Brokering Process Overview

1. An individual seller or other person has a reason to hold a note against a lump sum of payment owed.

    The most common forms of notes you will see are:

1st Mortgage Notes	2nd Mortgage Notes
Business Accounts	Receivables
Future Purchase Orders	Business Notes
Insurance Settlements	Life Insurance Policies
Annuities	Estate Inheritances
Lottery Winnings	Royalties
Automobile Notes	Recreational Vehicle Notes
Mobile Home Notes	Equipment Leases

Property Leases   Tax Line Certificates

Workers Compensation   Court Ordered Settlements and Payments

Note: The most common types of notes you will encounter early in your career will be those secured by either real or personal property. For instance, the 1st and 2nd mortgage note is a frequent component in the Note Brokering process. To simplify the process and promote clarity in the training course we will use the Mortgage Note in our examples. You should remember that the processes described apply to any situation in which periodic payments are made in exchange for a lump sum owed. We will review examples of potential types of notes you may broker in more detail later in the course.

Essentially, the concept you must keep in mind is that a note is ANY promise to repay. We will provide you with common examples that you will use as the starting basis for your business, but the success of a Note Broker hinges partially on the ability to source new and unusual note products.

2.   The Seller negotiates a sales price plus other payments such as interest accumulations and finance charges with the individual who will be making payments on the note.

3.   The Seller accepts periodic payments from the individual making payments on the note as negotiated in the contract.

4.   You contact the Seller, discuss their potential desire and need to obtain a cash lump sum settlement instead of the periodic payments that they are currently receiving.

Sellers are often forced to accept periodic payments in lieu of the lump sum sales price they were initially seeking.

This need is created when the cost of an item exceeds the amount the individual is able to offer to the seller to provide a cash settlement.

The seller will typically wish to obtain the lump sum cash they initially desired.

This becomes possible through the transfer the receipt of periodic payments to another individual, in this case the note investor.

5.   You obtain specific information regarding the parameters of the Seller's cash settlement needs and the details of the transaction negotiated at the creation of the note.

6.   You will obtain basic documentation that details the specifics of the note.

SKILL BUILDER: It is important to remember that you will be negotiating the cash out of the note at a discount off of the face value.

This is a necessity in a successful note transaction.

If there is no discount off of the face value of the note, the Investor will probably not obtain the return on investment that they require.

Many Sellers do not understand the discounting process.

It will be up to you to explain the methods Investors use to discount notes.

You must then encourage the Sellers to agree to accept a discounted figure in exchange for the benefits obtained through the obtainment of a cash settlement.

As the professional Note Broker, you must determine the best point in the negotiation process to discuss the actual transaction figures. The Chapter negotiating the sale will provide you with proven processes you will wish to incorporate into your negotiation strategy.

7.   You will review the documentation provided by the Seller against the target note parameters set by the Investor to determine the potential of the note. The notes potential as an investment will be discussed at length later in the course. For now, you must understand that some notes will be more desirable to potential Investors than other notes. This desirability is based on factors such as:

•   The term of the note

•   The interest accumulations assessed on the principal of the note

- The number of payments that have been made against the note

- The credit worthiness of the individual making periodic payments against the note

- Other factors will be determined as important depending on the specific note type and the Investor with whom you choose to work

Each Investor with whom you have a working relationship will have specific types of notes and terms they seek for their investment dollars. Part of being a professional Note Broker is gaining the ability to assess a note in comparison to the preferences of each of your Investor partners.

Once you have determined the Investor who will be most suited to the note you are reviewing you will begin the sale negotiation process.

8. You will contact the potential Investor to discuss the parameters of the note available for purchase. An essential point to understand is that there are effectively two career options available to you within the broader note-brokering venue.

Career A: Some Note Brokers simply notify the potential Investor of the existence of the note and the terms the Seller has stated they desire for the transfer of their interest in the note.

You, as the Note Broker will then receive a finder's fee and step away from the transaction.

The Investor reviews the parameters of the note to determine its potential and finalizes the negotiation and transfer of the note with the Seller.

Career B: Some Note Brokers maintain their position in the transaction. You would continue to fulfill the function of negotiator in the Note Brokering process. When you choose to perform this service, you will not provide either the Seller or potential Investor with specific contact information of the other party.

o   You will provide the basic note parameters and terms to the Investor.

- o   The Investor will assess the potential of the note and determine exactly what they are willing to pay to the Seller in exchange for the note.

- o   The Investor provides an offer of purchase to you.

- o   You will compare this offer of purchase terms requested by the seller.

In some cases, the terms offered by the Investor will exceed the terms stated as acceptable by the Seller. This provides another potential income source for you. We will explain this potential in more detail in the Chapter negotiating commission.

In other cases, the amount offered by the Investor will fall below the amount that the Seller has stated is an acceptable cash out figure. When this occurs, you will need to negotiate the settlement amount with the Seller or the offer amount with the Investor until a contract that is satisfactory to both parties can be created. If the parties cannot agree, you should remit the note to another investor. Each investor will have different criteria and requirements of the notes that they prefer. They will also have different discounting processes. This means that if the first negotiation process falls through, you have other options available.

The two options described may also be blended to incorporate both types of processes and income into your Note Brokering business.

9.   Once the terms agreed upon between the Seller and the Investor meet the requirements of each party, the deal can be finalized and proceed to settlement.

As a professionally trained Note Broker, you will have the opportunity to work with a variety of notes. Many people automatically think of the Mortgage Note when they hear the term Note Broker. It is true that Mortgage Notes are the most common item you will find, negotiate and broker during your career. The prevalence of credit issues, job interruptions and other factors that make it difficult for borrowers to qualify in the conventional mortgage market is creating a group of individuals who require seller held notes. This factor coupled with the increasing need for sellers to sell their property quickly due to job relocation, financial needs and other factors has created a climate in which seller held mortgage notes are commonplace. These notes are available in nearly every area of the country and the ability to negotiate a win-win transaction for both the Seller and the Investor is an attractive venue in which to work. However, as a Note Broker you do have other potential income streams, with which you can work and build your career. You should be aware that opportunity for your services exists in any situation in which periodic payments are being made against a lump sum of cash due.

Chapter

2

COMMON TYPES OF NOTES

When most individuals hear the term note, they think of the most common scenario in which notes are created, the real estate transaction. The reality is that any situation in which an individual holds the agreement to receive periodic payments of principal and other costs against an item sold or transferred is a note situation. Any note situation can be discounted and brokered to a note investor. The ability to source many types of notes will enable you to expand your business beyond that of your competition. In addition, the ability to facilitate the transfer of many forms of notes will enhance your reputation as the Note Broker who can do the job. This enhanced reputation will increase the potential referrals that you will receive. Increased referrals mean increased income!

First Mortgage Notes

First mortgage notes are created when a private buyer and a private seller enter a transaction in which the seller acts as the lender of the funds to purchase real property.

The funds are technically lent to a borrower and are secured against the real estate purchased.

The seller in this transaction performs much as a bank in a traditional mortgage loan.

The seller will set the terms and specifics of the note.

- The seller will pre-qualify the borrower to ensure a high probability that the buyer will pay the funds as agreed

- The seller will generate and record all required documents such as a note and mortgage agreement

- The seller will accept monthly payments of principal and interest

The mortgage note presents an attractive opportunity to Note Investors. The security level is high and the Investor has a strong probability of receiving the payments as agreed since the mortgage is typically linked to the primary residence or actual home of the individual making payments on the note.

Investors will assess the overall potential of the investment. In many situations, the Investor will have certain criteria that must be met.

- The type and condition of the collateral must be a rating of average or better as evidenced by a recent appraisal.

- The individuals making payments on the note must meet minimum credit and income eligibility criteria.

- The discount off the face value will be determined based on the

    Collateral condition

    Stability of the individual making payments

Length of time the payments remain due on the note

Interest rate negotiated on the note

Other considerations dependent on the specific transaction terms

- Proof must be provided showing that the borrower has made a minimum of five monthly payments as agreed under the note terms.

Other documentation may be required by the Investor based on the specific transaction being considered. More information regarding potential documentation and the reasons this documentation may be required is included in the pre-qualification Chapter.

Second Mortgage Notes

At times, a real estate seller will need to carry a second mortgage note on a property being sold and financed in the conventional market.

This carry back can occur for a variety of reasons and the two most common are

- The property appraisal may not have been equal to the sales price negotiated on the property.

- The lending institution financing the buyers may be unwilling to hold the full mortgage amount on the property due to specific borrower conditions that affect the risk levels of the borrower.

Each situation is different and the reasons the seller has chosen to hold a second mortgage against a conventionally financed property will be the first item of research when considering the brokering of this type of note.

A careful review of the appraisal on the property will be essential in second mortgage transactions.

- Investors require that the collateral securing the note be of equal or greater value than the amount financed against that collateral.

- A property that is over-financed may present additional risk to the Investor.

The stability and credibility of the borrower will be scrutinized more closely in the second mortgage transaction.

- By virtue of the second mortgage position, the capital investment of the Investor is at a greater risk.

- If the individual making payments on the note defaults, the funds received from the foreclosure against the property and the subsequent sale of the property will be distributed first to the taxing authorities, then to the holder of the first mortgage against that property. If there are funds left after paying these obligations, the Investor holding the second mortgage will obtain their funds from the remaining cash.

Other documentation may be required by the Investor based on the specific transaction being considered. More information regarding potential documentation and the specifics and purposes of the additional documentation requirements is included in the pre-qualification Chapter.

Business Finance Notes

Commercial notes or notes financing a business are slightly different from personal finance notes. The business note will be secured against the business assets and the ability of that business to operate in a profitable manner.

Seller financed business notes are created when the seller of a businesses holds the mortgage and note against a business. This will most often occur when the buyer of the business is unable to secure financing in the conventional market.

- A business note in a seller held transaction may or may not contain real estate as part of the transaction.

  When the transaction does not contain real estate the security to the Investor will typically be limited to only the creditworthiness of the buyer and the actual stock involved in the transaction.

- The Investor will usually require that they be the first lien holder against a business secured note.

This first lien position ensures that the Seller will receive the first payment if assets of the business must be liquidated to pay off the debts of that business.

- The Investor will scrutinize the credit report more carefully to assess the credit history of the individual making payments on the note. The Chapter, understanding the credit report, describes the criteria lenders use to make assessments regarding the probability that the borrower will make payments as agreed.

    The credit criteria for an under-secured business loan will typically require a nearly impeccable credit history both in the borrower's personal report and in any business credit history that is available.

- Since the Investor is providing money against the actual operation of the business, many Investors will require proof regarding the past profitability of the business.

    In seller held notes, this proof is typically provided by the seller who ran the business before the transfer occurred.

    This proof can be in the form of

    o   Federal Tax Returns

    o   A statement of profit and loss certified by an Accountant

- The Investor will also require that the individuals making payments on the note invest a larger amount of their own cash in the transaction.

    A standard is that the individual making payments on the note must invest a minimum of 35% of the sales price into the purchase.

    Often this investment will need to be proven as being provided from the borrowers own personal funds.

    The common belief in the note investment market is that the larger the investment of a buyer's own cash in the transaction the lower the risk of default.

    Proof that the funds were the borrower's own will need to be provided through third party documentation. This might include:

    o   Settlement Statements from a previous sale

o   Bank statements showing the existence of the funds used in the borrower's account

o   Proof of a 401K cash-out or other investment plans

o   Other documentation as is suitable based on the source of the borrower's down payment.

- The profitability of the business will be based, in part, on the borrower's ability to operate the business; the Investor will frequently require that the borrower provide proof of their ability to operate the business.

  The Investor will wish to research the items included on the borrower's resume, to ensure that the borrower has the experience needed to maintain the profitability of the business.

Other criteria will be determined on the individual Investor level. You must ensure you obtain all of the potential documentation that may be needed by the Investor to make a sound decision regarding the business investment.

Business Goods or Services Invoices - Net Billing

Many businesses offer a service known as net billing to their customers. This service allows the customer to obtain goods and services today and pay the bill 30, 45, 60 even 90 days from the date the goods or services are received. These credit terms allow the customer to purchase today on a revolving form of credit.

These invoices can actually be sold to an Investor.

- The Investor will provide immediate cash to the business providing the services or goods in exchange for these invoices.

- The Investor will purchase these invoices, sometimes the same day, for a discount of between 15% and 25% off the face value of the invoice.

  This is an excellent return for the Investor since the capital investment is expended for only a short period and the return, if the entire amount owed is received, is tremendous.

- The business owner benefits by having the immediate cash flow to reinvest the cash received into the fulfillment of more orders, negotiate cash transactions with the businesses own suppliers and other areas where an immediate cash flow can assist in business growth.

This process is commonly termed factoring. Many businesses around the country use factoring to ensure that the monthly cash flow received will meet their needs.

CAREER BUILDER: This sale of discounted invoices can actually generate repeat income for you.

Many Investors are willing to set up a daily or weekly invoice cash flow program. Some will even set up an immediate depository account between the business owner and the Investor. The invoices are forwarded to the Investor on a regulated basis and the negotiated cash value for each invoice will be immediately deposited in the business owner's account.

Other times the business owner will bundle a group of invoices due within stipulated periods into a package for submittal to the Investor. The Investor reviews the invoices to ensure that minimum qualification guidelines are met. They then forward the discounted value into the business owner's checking account.

Regardless of the process followed, you have the opportunity to negotiate residual commission with the Investor or the business owner for every invoice purchased.

Most Investors will want to review an application detailing:

- The business type

- Profitability

- Past credit performance of the business offering the invoices for purchase

- Other documents may be required and will be set by each individual Investor with whom you work.

Medical Receivables

Within the category of business receivables is a sub-category that should be considered as it can have a dramatic impact on the growth of your new business.

Medical receivables are billed in much the same net manner as with other businesses.

- Medical billing, even to insurance companies, can actually take a much longer time for payment to be received than other forms of business billings.

   Many doctors factor the term of payment into their billing requirements.

   The ability to obtain an immediate cash flow, even at the discounted rate offered by Investors, will appeal to many physicians' offices.

   > The physician must still make payments for items such as staff payroll, benefits programs, and rental or mortgage payments for their office location, insurance premiums, medical supplies, and many other items.

   > The doctor will frequently need to balance the projected inflow of cash against the expected outgo on a weekly or even daily basis in order to ensure smooth operations.

- The ability to provide a speedier cash flow creates a ready-made market for your new Note Brokering career.

Insurance Settlement Payments, Court Ordered Settlement and Payments

Court settlements, Insurance Settlements, Annuities, and other court ordered payments provide another potential for your Note Brokering businesses expansion. These types of settlements occur when a court order or a negotiated settlement requires an individual or company to make restitution for an accident, injury or other matter to another individual.

Many individuals opt for a structured settlement in which they receive a certain amount of their money on a monthly or installment basis over a period of years.

- These settlement payments are often structured over a period of 5, 10 even 20 years or longer.

- After a time, many individuals find they would have preferred a cash out in a lump sum rather than continued monthly payments.

- This cash out can allow the individual to move forward with their lives, paying obligations that have accumulated and investing the remainder of the funds in their future.

  o An individual receiving settlement payments can sell all or a portion of the settlement payments.

  o Federal and Statutory Law apply with regard to the term of payments that can be sold for a single cash premium.

  o Individuals can typically sell up to 20 years of expected settlement payments.

  o You, as the Note Broker, will usually negotiate a shorter sale of 5 or even 10 years against the payments.

This type of sale is very secure for the Investor because the courts often order the payments. In order to broker this type of note you will need to review the State Laws as they apply to the sales of settlement payments within the State where you plan to act as a Broker.

In order for the Investor to make a sound decision regarding the investment, they will usually require a copy of

- The order for payments

- Any contracts negotiated and implemented between the parties to the payments

- A breakdown of the payments that have been received

Lottery Winnings Payments

Similar to settlement payments many lottery winners will choose to accept periodic payments for their winnings rather than receive one lump sum. Many lottery programs offer either a lump sum at a substantial discount or a periodic pay out of funds that totals a much higher end figure.

- A high percentage of lottery winners initially choose the periodic payment option seeing the total of all sums paid as worth the wait for their money. Over time, the winner may find they have a financial need for a larger lump sum to accomplish their goals or a desire for a lump sum to fulfill their dreams.

- These payments are very secure and the Investor will typically be willing to purchase all or just a portion of the payments the lottery winner is owed at a discount off of the total payments expected.

In this scenario, the Investor is again receiving their return only in the discount portion of the negotiation.

- The Investor will require documentation outlining the payment terms and the total sums due under the winner agreement.

- The Investor will also require a breakdown of the payments already received against the winnings.

The lottery winner will receive the discounted lump sum for the number of payments they wish to sell now. Some lottery winners only wish to sell 2 or 3 years worth of expected payments while others have a larger financial need and wish to sell all of the remaining payments. It is up to you as the professional Note Broker to review the needs of the lottery winner and assist in negotiating the best possible transaction for all parties.

Expanded Opportunity

The items described in this Chapter are only the very beginning of the potential items you may pursue for your Note Brokering career. You should be constantly aware of other opportunities that exist around you each day. Some other potential sources of income for you include:

- Inheritances

- Lease Payments

- Personal Property sold under a note agreement between private individuals

- Retirement or Disability Payments due

- Reverse Mortgage Structured Programs

- Royalty Payments

- Senior Life Settlements

- Secured Property such as a vehicle or other goods sold under a note between

- Private individuals

- Vertical Settlements

- Winnings from Casino Games or other games of chance

Essentially any situation where a periodic payment is being made toward a lump sum owed is an opportunity in your new note-brokering career. We will focus our examples on real estate since this tends to be the most common and profitable Note Brokering opportunity. You should still consider the other possibilities available to you for the expansion of your business. Note Brokering opportunities exist all around you each day and as you gain confidence and knowledge, you will begin to see the potential opportunities to generate income through the transfer of all types of notes.

Chapter

3

SELLING FACTORS OF A NOTE

An integral portion of your new career is to locate potential notes and screen the note for factors that will be of interest to the investor. To complete the screening task, you must understand the elements of a note that will attract potential investors.

A salable note will contain three common factors:

1.   The note must contain an income stream.

     An income stream is defined as the periodic payments agreed to and accepted against a lump sum of money due.

2.   The note must have the ability to generate an income for the Investor.

     Note income is typically generated through two methods:

Discounting the Lump Sum

The note must contain an ability to obtain the income stream at a discount.

What this means is that the face value or total sum owed on a note must be more than the amount the Investor will pay the Seller for the privilege of accepting the payments due on a note.

A note without interest payments can still be viewed as a positive-growth investment if the amount the Investor pays for the note is lower than the amount the Investor will receive through the collection of monthly payments against the note.

Interest Payments on the Note Value

Most notes are written with a condition that the individual paying the note will make interest payments on the note balance.

This interest compensates the holder of the note for the time they will have to wait for a full return of the monies owed.

The Investor will typically make a lump-sum cash payment less the discount to the Seller against only the face value of the note.

The Investor will then be the individual who requires interest compensation against the monies due to them under the note.

The accumulation of interest can dramatically increase the amount of profit gained by holding a note.

The Investor will always factor the discounted purchase price of the note AND the sum total of interest expected against the note when calculating their overall income potential or returns on investment in the note.

3. The security of the note

The note is only as valuable as its ability to generate a positive cash flow.

Most Investors will wish to assess the probability that the payments due under the note agreement will be paid in a timely manner and in compliance with the terms of the note.

Many of the notes you will broker will be secured.

- The Investor is typically not interested in obtaining the actual property securing the note.

- Most Investors are placing their capital in an attempt to obtain a cash on cash return on their investment.

The Investor's interests in the note must be protected through a careful assessment of the stability of the individual making the note payments and the probability that this individual will make the payments as stipulated in the agreement. We will review qualifying criteria later in the course. For now, you must understand that a marketable note must contain a solid probability that the note will be paid or the Investor will be accepting a higher level of risk through the purchase of the note.

- The criteria you will review provides vital insight into the history of the borrower.

- This information allows the Investor to assess the borrower's future performance potential. However, you must remember that it is not possible to assess the probability of a borrower default with 100% accuracy.

- Unique situations do arise that might cause a previously stable borrower to default on a note. When this occurs, the property against which the note is secured becomes a factor.

The Investor will wish to confirm the value and the condition of the property securing the note. To do this they will need to review any appraisal completed on the property securing the note. The appraisal will provide the Investor with

- The perceived value of the property

- Information regarding the condition of the property

- The growth and condition of the neighborhood in which the property is located

- Other information that will assist the Investor in determining their potential ability to regain their investment capital from the sale of the property if the individual making payments on the note should default

A Chapter designed to assist you in understanding the appraisal documents is included later in the course. You must fully comprehend the security the property provides to the Investor and items that will appear as red flags to any Investor considering an investment in the note package you are presenting.

THE NOTE SELLER

Note Sellers will frequently take a note on a receivable or a home because the buyer is unable to provide the seller with a total cash-out at the time of purchase. This is called 'creative financing' and is a very profitable investment opportunity. However, many sellers were not looking for an investment opportunity when they sold their home or other items; they were looking for a straight cash sale. Sometimes situations exist which cause the seller to agree to hold a note against the purchase and accept monthly payments from the buyer toward that note.

In a real estate transaction, the seller may agree to hold a note for many different reasons.

Speed of Sale: In a soft real estate market offering creative or seller held financing might allow the seller to sell their property more quickly than other real estate offerings on the market.

Sell for More: A soft real estate market is also often termed a buyer's market because there are typically more properties for sale than there are buyers to buy them. This tends to drive the average sales price down and causes a loss for the seller. Through the act of holding the note on the property, the seller is typically able to command a higher sales price for the transaction.

Source More Buyers: Offering creative financing options during any real estate market conditions opens up a new group of buyers who might not otherwise be home shopping. These buyers are the ones who, for a variety of reasons, do not qualify for conventional financing methods. These buyers will typically pay a premium price for a property simply for the opportunity to purchase, regardless of the conventional market conditions.

The ability to work with these additional buyers will also increase the potential sales speed because of the additional buyer base to which the seller can market.

Earn Interest: Sellers receive the interest earnings that typically go to the banks in conventional transactions. These interest earnings are what make financing institutions so profitable.

Through seller financing, sellers of real estate are now able to obtain some of that profit for themselves.

The addition of interest earnings can dramatically increase the overall profit margin received from a property. Even a quick glance at an amortization schedule will show how much money is paid in interest on a yearly basis. The interest earnings are one of the factors that make the purchase of the note attractive to Investors.

Regardless of the reasons the seller originally agreed to hold the note on the purchase, most sellers would have preferred a cash settlement. This creates an excellent opportunity for you to broker this note.

- The Investor will gain the opportunity to generate a return on their investment through the simple discounting of the face value of the note as well as the collection of the negotiated interest payments and other finance charges.

- The Seller will gain the lump sum of cash they initially desired. This lump sum of cash provides the Seller with the opportunity to settle debt, fulfill personal goals and begin securing their future with a single lump sum rather than waiting for the periodic payments to accumulate to the lump sum figure necessary to obtain their goals.

- The person making payments on the note does not perceive any difference in the transaction except for the location to which they send the monthly payment.

All parties walk away from the transaction feeling satisfied with their gains in the deal.

Chapter 5

THE INVESTOR

*Any individual looking to place sums of capital in
an investment is doing so in an attempt to obtain the
highest possible return on their investment dollars.
A note investor is an investor who is capitalizing on
the ability of discounted notes to increase the return
on their investment dollars though lower-risk
investments. These investors will enter the note
purchase arena for a variety of reason.*

- Many people are seeking investment opportunities to secure their future.

- Some are concerned with dwindling retirement benefits.

- Others are simply hoping to gain a substantial return with which to improve the quality of their lives.

Regardless of their specific motivations, the primary goal of every Investor is the same, the highest return on the funds placed while maintaining a level of security that keeps their initial investment dollars safe.

The purchase of notes accomplishes both the primary and the specific goals of the Investor. If the note is properly screened to insure the terms and specifics of the note fall with in the risk parameters established by the Investor and proven through years of note performance assessment, the capital investment retains a high level of security.

The investor obtains a high return rate on their investment capital through the process of

- Interest application

- Finance charge accumulation

- Note discount negotiation

Note Discount

The first item to understand is the note discounting process.

The note discount process is similar to a loan to value assessment completed by conventional lenders.

1. Investors will assess the potential gains and potential risks of each note.

2. From this assessment, they will determine the maximum they can safely invest in a particular note and still maintain that level of security and high return necessary to make the transaction beneficial to them.

Example:	Original Note:	$45,000.00
	Principal Payments Received:	$ 4,789.00

Current Face Value:	$43,511.00
Risk Level Assessment:	12% default risk
Discount:	$ 5,221.32
Note Cash-out Offer	$38,289.68

The note cash-out offer is the potential cash figure the Investor might offer to the seller.

3. The seller receives a large lump sum.

Granted the cash out received is not equal to the face value of the note but the seller obtains the ability to use the lump funds immediately rather than accepting the funds in the form of monthly payments over a long period of time.

4. The Investor has gained an immediate equity position in the note.

This immediate equity position offsets the risk the Investor is taking by placing their funds against the note.

The equity generated through the discount also increases the return the Investor will receive if the individual making payments on the note completes the contract agreement as outlined.

Example: The immediate assumed return on their investment the Investor will perceive is 12% return.

In other words, they will obtain a 12% positive cash flow from the placement of their money.

12% is an incredible return for an investment.

This is the primary reason note investing has become an attractive option in the investment community.

Note Interest

The Investor will gain a second method of return the Investor will review is the return generated through interest and finance charges negotiated in the original note agreement.

- When a seller agrees to hold a note against the sale of a piece of property, the buyer and seller will typically agree to a certain amount of interest payments as compensation to the seller for holding the paper on the purchase.

- When the note is sold to an Investor the Investor obtains the rights to the interest payments due under the note terms.

  The interest rate that can be obtained through the purchase of a creatively financed note can truly benefit the Investor.

  Collecting interest is one of the primary reasons that banks are so successful and profitable. When you calculate the total of the sales price plus the monthly interest payments, you will see that the actual cash return obtained for the property increases dramatically.

To see what a great benefit it is to the investor to obtain a higher interest rate note, use an amortization calculator to assess different value notes and the potential interest accumulation over the life of those notes. You will quickly see that in a standard amortization, the first payments on a property are primarily applied to interest. What this means to the Investor is that they will obtain a maximum return on their investment early in the loan term.

This application of interest early in the payment process allows the Investor to obtain the desired return on their investment dollars even in a situation where the individual making payments on the note refinances with a conventional lender after the Investor has purchased the note. The face value discount negotiated also provides an immediate return to the Investor in case of a refinance situation.

The following chart and explanation provide more information to aid you in better understanding interest accumulations.

Principal borrowed: $102000.00

Annual Payments: 12   **Total Payments:** 360

Annual interest rate: 6.50%   **Periodic interest rate:** 0.5417%

Regular Payment amount: $644.71   **Final Balloon Payment:** $0.00

Note: the following numbers are estimates. See the amortization schedule for more accurate values.

Total Repaid: $232095.60

Total Interest Paid: $130095.60

Interest as percentage of Principal: 127.545%

Payment	Principal	Interest	Cum Prin	Cum Int	Prin Bal
1	92.21	552.50	92.21	552.50	101907.79
2	92.71	552.00	184.92	1104.50	101815.08
3	93.21	551.50	278.13	1656.00	101721.87
4	93.72	550.99	371.85	2206.99	101628.15
5	94.22	550.49	466.07	2757.48	101533.93
6	94.73	549.98	560.80	3307.46	101439.20
7	95.25	549.46	656.05	3856.92	101343.95
8	95.76	548.95	751.81	4405.87	101248.19
9	96.28	548.43	848.09	4954.30	101151.91
10	96.80	547.91	944.89	5502.21	101055.11
11	97.33	547.38	1042.22	6049.59	100957.78
12	97.86	546.85	1140.08	6596.44	100859.92

13	98.39	546.32	1238.47	7142.76	100761.53
14	98.92	545.79	1337.39	7688.55	100662.61
15	99.45	545.26	1436.84	8233.81	100563.16
16	99.99	544.72	1536.83	8778.53	100463.17
17	100.53	544.18	1637.36	9322.71	100362.64
18	101.08	543.63	1738.44	9866.34	100261.56
19	101.63	543.08	1840.07	10409.42	100159.93
20	102.18	542.53	1942.25	10951.95	100057.75
21	102.73	541.98	2044.98	11493.93	99955.02
22	103.29	541.42	2148.27	12035.35	99851.73
23	103.85	540.86	2252.12	12576.21	99747.88
24	104.41	540.30	2356.53	13116.51	99643.47

25	104.97	539.74	2461.50	13656.25	99538.50
26	105.54	539.17	2567.04	14195.42	99432.96
27	106.11	538.60	2673.15	14734.02	99326.85
28	106.69	538.02	2779.84	15272.04	99220.16
29	107.27	537.44	2887.11	15809.48	99112.89
30	107.85	536.86	2994.96	16346.34	99005.04
31	108.43	536.28	3103.39	16882.62	98896.61
32	109.02	535.69	3212.41	17418.31	98787.59
33	109.61	535.10	3322.02	17953.41	98677.98
34	110.20	534.51	3432.22	18487.92	98567.78
35	110.80	533.91	3543.02	19021.83	98456.98
36	111.40	533.31	3654.42	19555.14	98345.58

37	112.00	532.71	3766.42	20087.85	98233.58
38	112.61	532.10	3879.03	20619.95	98120.97
39	113.22	531.49	3992.25	21151.44	98007.75
40	113.83	530.88	4106.08	21682.32	97893.92
41	114.45	530.26	4220.53	22212.58	97779.47
42	115.07	529.64	4335.60	22742.22	97664.40
43	115.69	529.02	4451.29	23271.24	97548.71
44	116.32	528.39	4567.61	23799.63	97432.39
45	116.95	527.76	4684.56	24327.39	97315.44
46	117.58	527.13	4802.14	24854.52	97197.86
47	118.22	526.49	4920.36	25381.01	97079.64
48	118.86	525.85	5039.22	25906.86	96960.78

49	119.51	525.20	5158.73	26432.06	96841.27
50	120.15	524.56	5278.88	26956.62	96721.12
51	120.80	523.91	5399.68	27480.53	96600.32
52	121.46	523.25	5521.14	28003.78	96478.86
53	122.12	522.59	5643.26	28526.37	96356.74
54	122.78	521.93	5766.04	29048.30	96233.96
55	123.44	521.27	5889.48	29569.57	96110.52
56	124.11	520.60	6013.59	30090.17	95986.41
57	124.78	519.93	6138.37	30610.10	95861.63
58	125.46	519.25	6263.83	31129.35	95736.17
59	126.14	518.57	6389.97	31647.92	95610.03
60	126.82	517.89	6516.79	32165.81	95483.21

Example: The first factor to review is the total interest paid.

In this scenario, the items are amortized over a period of 30 years.

Total Repaid:	$232,095.60
Total Interest Paid:	$130,095.60
Actual Sales Price:	$102,000.00

Between principal and interest payments, the Seller may actually receive $232,095.60 dollars in return for their initial investment of 102,000.

The factor to remember is that the typical borrower will not remain in the mortgage for the entire finance term.

The Investor will assess the total perceived interest earnings and the average term a borrower will typically keep a home or mortgage.

This average is usually assessed at five years.

This means the Investor has the potential to gain the full interest earnings due on the note but will frequently earn only those interest accumulations that become due in the first five years of the note term.

This potential refinance will dramatically affect the potential return to the Investor and is often a factor in the actual discount rate the Investor applies to the note offer.

Chapter

6

BUILDING A QUALIFIED PACKAGE

A professional Note Broker will always provide the potential Investor with a complete, qualified note package. To provide a complete and qualified investment package you must understand the various documents that you will gather and provide to the Investor. Each document you provide contains essential information that the Investor will need to assess the viability of a particular note investment.

Before presenting your first package to an Investor, you must comprehend the information conveyed by each document in the package.

Some documents will provide specific details regarding the profitability of a note.

Other documents contain information that assists the Investor in determining the security of the note.

The documents of interest to the Investor will include items such as:

PACKAGE DETAILS

The Note
A copy of the actual note that will be transferred enables the investor to see the negotiated terms of the original transaction

The Mortgage
The mortgage or other security instrument shows the property against which the note is secured.

The Settlement Statement
The HUD 1 or Settlement Statement details the actual specifics of the transaction between the note seller and the individual making payments on the note

Amortization Schedules
Amortization Schedules provide a detailed breakdown of the specific payments, status and place in the transaction where the note investor will gain an interest.

Two amortization schedules will usually be necessary when documenting a note package.

The first amortization schedule will be based upon the initial note negotiations.

The second amortization schedule should be generated based upon the actual payments, penalties and other amounts applied to the transaction since the original note was created. This second schedule provides a specific breakdown of what the investor is actually obtaining if they choose to purchase the note.

Appraisal
An appraisal of the property that shows the estimated value of the property, the condition of the property and other factors that influences the final value of the property.

Proof of hazard insurance Hazard insurance coverage provides security to the investor that if an event occurs that damages the property and potentially lowers the value of the security, the damages will be repaired and therefore the investor's interests will be protected.

Title Binder or Insurance If a title search was conducted on the property the Investor will wish to see a copy of the title search or a statement of title insurance obtained because of the search.

This proof of clear title protects the Investor from others claiming an interest in the property at some future point in time. This claimed interest could result in an elevated risk to the Investor.

Other documents may be determined as important to the qualification process by the specific Investor with whom you plan to place the note. These documents are explained more fully in later Chapters.

CREDITWORTHINESS

Other documents will be requested that provide details regarding the stability of the note or the probability the note will be paid as agreed. These documents include items that show the creditworthiness of the individual making payments on the note such as:

Income Proof and stability of the income earned by the individuals making payments on the note will be a critical factor influencing the probability that the note will be repaid as agreed.

Both the income amount and the percentage of income spent on debt can affect the probability the borrower will perform the obligations outlined in the note.

Payment History Proof that the payments required under the note have been made as agreed will be required.

The amortization schedule will show the impact each payment had on the principal amount owed, the interest accumulation and other items.

The Investor will also wish to see proof that the payments have been made as outlined. This provides further assurance to the Investor regarding the stability of the borrower.

Credit Report A recent credit report on the individuals making payments on the note will often be required.

The Investor will wish to review the credit history of the individuals making payments on the note.

This history will provide information to the Investor regarding the probability that the borrower will continue to make the payments as agreed under the note.

Derogatory Explanation An explanation for any derogatory information appearing on the report may be required depending on the specific situation.

Other documents that provide information regarding the individuals making payments on the note may be requested by specific Investors based on their qualification criteria. These documents are explained more fully in later Chapters.

You must gather documentation that the investor will use to scrutinize potential notes.

- A comprehensive understanding of the note package documentation is vital to your career success.

- The more adept you become at documenting potential packages and at qualifying those packages, the easier it will be for you to locate Investors who will wish to review that package.

- Gaining a reputation with your investment partners as the Note Broker who always submits solid, complete packages will enhance your career success and your working relationships with these Investors.

Investors see hundreds, even thousands of potential investment packages each year. The Investor is interested in the bottom line of the packages.

- A properly documented and qualified package can save the Investor hours of effort during the pre-qualification process.

- This is essential to ensuring that your packages are always welcome in the office of the potential Investor.

- The better prepared your packages are the higher the likelihood that your packages will be placed on the top of the review stack.

The following documentation checklist is a good basic checklist of items you should request from the holder of the note at the first interview. Each situation and each note will be different so some situations will require you to request additional or even alternate documentation. The following checklist provides you with the most common items you will need to gather and assess before you offer your first package to a potential Investor partner.

SUBMISSION SHEET

Broker: _____ Package ID:_____ Date: _____

___ Copy Original Note

___ Copy Original Security Instrument, Type _____

___ Settlement Statement

___ Original Amortization Schedule

___ Schedule of Payments Made

___ Modified Amortization Schedule

___ Proof that payments have been made as agreed

___ Credit report

___ Consent for credit check

___ Recent Appraisal

___ Proof of Insurance

___ Analysis Worksheet

___ Negotiation Checklist

___ Other _____

___ Other _____

Figure 6:1 – Form - Sample Submission Sheet

THE NOTE

Holding a note is not as complicated as many people believe. A property seller will act just like a bank or other lending institution involved in a note transaction. The seller will:

- Negotiate the sales price and terms

- Pre-qualify the buyer.

- Create an agreement for the sale of the item.

- Negotiate the repayment plan the buyer feels able to afford.

  The repayment plan will include a payment toward the principal amount the buyer must pay to compensate the seller for the actual goods.

  The repayment plan will typically also include a premium called interest or a finance charge.

  This interest or finance charge compensates the seller for the time they must wait to obtain their full amount of cash.

  The interest accumulation or finance charge also provides the seller with a profit return on their lent funds to offset any risk of buyer default.

An important concept to understand is that the seller is actually lending money just as if the seller were the bank or funding company. Many people do not look at the concept of seller-financed notes as the seller actually lending money since no actual cash changes hands.

- The cash value of the item being sold using seller financing is worth a certain cash premium.

- The note the seller and buyer create actually becomes a cash instrument.

- This instrument is of interest to Investors in the Note Brokering process.

Throughout this course, it is important that you consistently view the note as an actual stack of cash. Viewing the note as cash promotes an understanding of some of the processes that we will review throughout the course.

Many factors will affect the potential value of the note. When we say potential value, we are not discussing the actual face value or amount owed on the note we are referring to the amount the Investor will perceive the note as being worth to them. We have explained that the Investor will need to negotiate a discount off of the face value of the note in an effort to increase the security of their investment as well as to generate a higher rate of return.

NOTE DETAILS

If the buyer and the seller agree to a sale that requires the seller to hold a mortgage on the property it is common practice to draw up both a mortgage document and a promissory note.

A promissory note is a contract between the borrower and the lender. In the case of seller financing, the lender is actually the seller. Often simply referred to as a note, the document must contain certain key components to ensure it is legally binding and enforceable.

- The note must be in writing.

- The note must be between a borrower and a lender who have the ability to enter a legally binding contract.

- The note states the borrowers promise to pay a certain sum of money and the terms under which those monies will be paid.

- The borrower signs the document and the completed note is given to the seller acting as the lender.

Promissory notes need not be complicated but they must clearly outline the terms under which the loan is being granted. Terms could include:

- the principal amount of the mortgage

- the interest rate agreed upon

- the date payment is due

- the late charge, if any, incurred when a payment is paid beyond the due date

- the date which these late charges are assessed

- the length of time payments shall be made

- how the payments will be credited on the account for example to interest and then principal

- any other details which have been negotiated between the buyer and the seller with regards to the repayment of the agreed to monies

Simply put a promissory note is the written promise to repay a debt and acceptable terms and methods for those payments.

The promissory note is the actual product whose transfer you will be negotiating.

The details of the note will provide both you and the Investor with much of the basic pre-qualification information the Investor will review with regard to note profitability. The following example incorporates all of the basic note requirements. The notes you will work with may vary in form from the examples but will incorporate all of the basic components you will see in this example.

Promissory Installment Note (w/Balloon Payment)

Date: _____ *(insert date)*

Borrower: _____ *(insert buyer(s) name)*

Borrower's Address: _____ *(insert buyer's new address)*

Payee: _____ *(insert seller(s) name)*

Place for Payment _____ *(insert seller(s) mailing address)*

Principal Amount: $_____ *(insert total loan amount)* Term: _____ *(insert number of payments)*

Monthly Payments: $_____ *(insert total of payment)*   _____ *(insert number of months)*

1. INTEREST RATE

Annual interest rate on matured, unpaid amounts shall be _____% (_____)
(insert interest rate).

2. PAYMENT TERMS

This Note is due and payable as follows, _____ (_____) *(insert number of payments)* equal monthly payments of $_____ principal and interest *(insert monthly payment amount).*

The first such payment due and payable on the 1st day of _____, 20____, and a like installment shall be due and payable on the same day of each succeeding month thereafter until the total principal of $_____ principal *(insert total principal amount)* is paid in full.

If each payment is not paid on time, the remaining balance will be subject to the maximum amount of interest permitted by the Laws of the Commonwealth of _____. *(insert applicable State)*

3. BALLOON PAYMENT.

Borrower promises to make a single, final payment for the entire balance owed to the Payee on or before _____ *(due date for balloon payment).*

4. BORROWER'S PRE-PAYMENT RIGHT

Borrower reserves the right to prepay this Note in whole or in part, prior to maturity, without penalty.

Figure 6:2 – Sample Promissory Note – Pg 1

5. PLACE FOR PAYMENT

Borrower promises to pay to the order of Payee at the place for payment and according to the terms for payment the principal amount plus interest at the rates stated above. All unpaid amounts shall be due by the final scheduled payment date.

6. DEFAULT AND ACCELERATION CLAUSE

If Borrower defaults in the payment of this Note or in the performance of any obligation, and the default continues after Payee gives Borrower notice of the default and the time within which it must be cured, as may be required by law or written agreement, then Payee may declare the unpaid principal balance and earned interest on this Note immediately due. Borrower and each surety, endorser, and guarantor waive all demands for payment, presentation for payment, notices of intentions to accelerate maturity, notices of acceleration of maturity, protests, and notices of protest, to the extent permitted by law.

7. INTEREST ON PAST DUE INSTALLMENTS AND CHARGES

All past due installments of principal and/or interest and/or all other past-due incurred charges shall bear interest after maturity at the maximum amount of interest permitted by the Laws of the Commonwealth of _____ until paid. Failure by Borrower to remit any payment by the 15th day following the date that such payment is due entitles the Payee hereof to declare the entire principal and accrued interest immediately due and payable. Payee's forbearance in enforcing a right or remedy, as set forth herein shall not be deemed a waiver of said right or remedy for a subsequent cause, breach or default of the Borrower's obligations herein.

8. INTEREST

Interest on this debt evidenced by this Note shall not exceed the maximum amount of non-usurious interest that may be contracted for, taken, reserved, charged, or

received under law; any interest in excess of the maximum shall be credited on the principal of the debt or, if that has been paid, refunded. On any acceleration or required or permitted prepayment, any such excess shall be canceled automatically as of the acceleration or prepayment or, if already paid, credited on the principal of

Figure 6:3 – Sample Promissory Note – Pg 2

the debt or, if the principal of the debt has been paid, refunded. This provision overrides other provisions in this instrument (and any other instruments) concerning this debt.

9. FORM OF PAYMENT

Any check, draft, Money Order, or other instrument given in payment of all or any portion hereof may be accepted by the holder and handled in collection in the customary manner, but the same shall not constitute payment hereunder or diminish any rights of the holder hereof except to the extent that actual cash proceeds of such instruments are unconditionally received by the payee and applied to this indebtedness in the manner elsewhere herein provided.

10. ATTORNEY'S FEES

If this Note is given to an attorney for collection or enforcement, or if suit is brought for collection or enforcement, or if it is collected or enforced through probate, bankruptcy, or other judicial proceeding, then Borrower shall pay Payee all costs of collection and enforcement, including reasonable attorney's fees and court costs in addition to other amounts due.

11. SEVERABILITY

If any provision of this Note or the application thereof shall, for any reason and to any extent, be invalid or unenforceable, neither the remainder of this Note nor the application of the provision to other persons, entities or circumstances shall be affected thereby, but instead shall be enforced to the maximum extent permitted by law.

12. BINDING EFFECT

The covenants, obligations and conditions herein contained shall be binding on and inure to the benefit of the heirs, legal representatives, and assigns of the parties hereto.

13. DESCRIPTIVE HEADINGS

The descriptive headings used herein are for convenience of reference only and they are not intended to have any affect whatsoever in determining the rights or obligations under this Note.

Figure 6:3 – Sample Promissory Note – Pg 3

14. CONSTRUCTION

The pronouns used herein shall include, where appropriate, either gender or both, singular and plural.

15. GOVERNING LAW

This Note shall be governed, construed and interpreted by, through and under the Laws of the Commonwealth of _____.
Borrower is responsible for all obligations represented by this Note.

EXECUTED this _____ day of _____, 20_____.

Borrower's Signature: _____

Borrower's Printed or Typed Name: _____

Figure 6:4 – Sample Promissory Note – Pg 4

Figure - This form is included for example purposes only. The form is modified from the acceptable real estate forms as released by HUD. The services of a real estate professional should be retained to ensure the correct forms are used for your transaction.

The components of the example promissory note allow certain rights to be legally enforced on the part of both the buyer and the seller.

This promissory note is explained as follows:

- State that the document is a promissory note

- Give the location and the date of the notes signing. As with any contract, the location stated in the contract establishes which state laws govern the execution of the document

- State that the borrower has received something of value and in return, promises to pay the debt as described in the note

- Identify who is to receive the payments

- Show where the borrower is to send or make said payments

- Show the amount of funds for which the note is being signed

- Show the interest rate on the debt

- State the date from which interest will be charged and payments shall begin

- Show the amount of the payments to be made including principal and interest

- State the prepayment decision. Prepayment of all or part of the loan funds prior to a specified date is sometimes penalized as part of the negotiation process

  Prepayment penalty regulations vary by state and if a prepayment penalty is to be imposed on a loan, the applicable laws should be fully researched.

- Indicate the grace period, if any, provided to the borrower before the addition of a late-charge to the payment

- Clarify exactly how the payments remitted shall be applied. In this instance, all payments are applied first to the interest currently accumulated with the remainder of the payment applied to the principal balance owing on the loan.

- Provide the lender the right to accelerate the loan and demand immediate payment of all interest and principal owed if the borrower misses any individual payments. This clause allows the acceleration to be at the lender decision.

- Cause the borrower to agree to pay any costs incurred by the lender if the borrower falls behind on the payments.

If the promissory note is tied to a mortgage, the mortgage document is referenced in the note. This makes the note a secured loan. Without this reference, the note would be considered an unsecured personal loan or unsecured note.

The borrower signs the note and is sometimes referred to as the note maker. If two or more persons sign the note, it is common to include a statement in the note that the borrowers are jointly and severally making the note. This means that the terms of the note and the obligations created are enforceable on the makers as a group or upon each note maker individually.

If the note is tied to a mortgage, the property being held as security in the note will be referenced and at times, it will be described. The Investor does not wish to be in a situation where the security against which the note is held is repossessed or foreclosed due to a default. However, the fact that the security exists can play a large role in the assessment of risk the Investor will perform on each potential note investment.

This security instrument may be in the form of a mortgage, trust deed or promissory contract. The security instrument is what legally binds the item put up as security against the debt. Most transactions you will see early in your career will be the seller held mortgages. This Mortgage will define the actual legal obligations of the note and the Seller and will contain the specifics regarding the methods in which the Seller may recover their investment in the event of a borrower default through the taking of the property named. The mortgage or other security instrument may take many forms. The basic components will always remain similar. It is important that you understand the components of a mortgage note so that you may pre-qualify the package before submitting it to an Investor partner.

THE MORTGAGE

Financing transactions that contain real estate are typically secured in the form of a mortgage.

A mortgage causes the note to be secured against real property rather than other property or as an unsecured personal loan. Typically, a seller will utilize both a note and a mortgage in the real estate transactions in which you are brokering the note.

- The note is the promise to repay the funds.

- A mortgage is a separate agreement from the note and provides the security or collateral in case of non-payment.

The key components of a mortgage include the act of putting the property as collateral and the conditions under which the buyer will maintain the collateral to protect the interest of the Investor or Seller while the note is payable.

The following page contains an example of a simplified mortgage. This example will illustrate all of the basic requirements needed to create a legally binding document. The validity and contents of the mortgage agreement is vital to the Investor. The mortgage provides the Investor with the ability to regain their capital through a foreclosure and subsequent sale in the event the borrower defaults on the payments agreed to within the note.

MORTGAGE

This mortgage made this _____ day of _____ between _____
hereinafter called Mortgagor, and _____ hereinafter called
Mortgagee.

Whereas, the Mortgagor is indebted to the Mortgagee in the principal sum of
_____ dollars payable _____ as
evidenced by the Mortgagor's note of the same date as this mortgage, hereinafter called
Note.

To secure the Mortgagee the repayment of the indebtedness evidenced by said Note, with
interest thereon; the Mortgagor does hereby mortgage, grant and convey to the Mortgagee
the following described property in the County of _____ State of _____.

Lot ____, Block _____, as shown on Page _____ of Deed Book _____ filed with the
County Recorder of said County and State.

Furthermore, the Mortgagor fully warrants the title to said land and will defend the same
against the lawful claims of all persons.

If the Mortgagor, his heirs, legal representatives or assigns pay unto the Mortgagee, all
sums due by said Note then this mortgage and the estate created shall hereby cease and be
null and void.

Until said note is fully paid, the Mortgagor agrees to pay all taxes on said land and the
Mortgagor agrees not to remove or demolish building or other improvements on the
mortgaged land without the approval of the Mortgagee.

The mortgagor agrees to carry adequate homeowners insurance to protect the Mortgagee in
case of damage or destruction of the mortgaged property.

The Mortgagor agrees to keep the mortgaged property in good repair and not permit waste
or deterioration of the property.

It is further agreed that the Mortgagee shall have the right to inspect the mortgaged
property as may be necessary for the security of the Note.

Figure 6:5 – Sample Mortgage – Pg 1

If the Mortgagor does not abide by this Mortgage or the accompanying Note, the Mortgagee may declare the entire unpaid balance on the Note immediately due and payable.

If the Mortgagor sells or otherwise conveys title to the mortgaged property, the Mortgagee may declare the entire unpaid balance on the Note immediately due and payable.

If all or part of the Mortgaged property is taken by act of eminent domain, any sums of money received shall be applied to the Note.

In WITNESS WHEREOF, the Mortgagor has executed this mortgage.

_____

Mortgagor

Figure 6:6 – Sample Mortgage – Pg 2

This form is included for example purposes only. The form is modified from the acceptable real estate forms as released by HUD. The services of a real estate professional should be retained to ensure the correct forms are used for your transaction.

Mortgage Key

The first item on a mortgage is the date of its making and the names of the parties involved.

- Mortgagor refers to the person who owes the mortgage

- Mortgagee refers to the person or company who is receiving the payments from the mortgage more commonly referred to as the lender.

The debt for which the mortgage is being held as collateral is named.

The borrower of the funds conveys their interest in the property being held as collateral to the lender.

The mortgaged property is then described.

The borrower states that the property being provided as collateral legally belongs to them and that the borrower will be responsible for defending ownership against all other claims of interest by other parties. The seller or lender will want to verify this through a title search and, at times, will require the buyer to carry title insurance as a protection against any future claims to the title by other parties.

- This is known as the defeasance clause and it contains provisions to nullify and make void the mortgage when the note has been paid in full.

The borrower makes certain promises to the lender, which protect the collateral or property that acts as security for the loan. These are frequently termed covenants.

- Covenant to pay taxes is the borrower's agreement to pay the property taxes on the mortgaged property. This is an important factor for the lender because if the taxes are not paid they may create a lien on the property that is superior to the lien held by the lender. This means that the property may be foreclosed upon and sold for the repayment of past due taxes. This possibility places the lender position at risk.

- Covenant against removal prohibits the borrower from removing or demolishing any building or improvement on the property. Demolishing or removing improvements may reduce the value of the collateral offered to the lender against the note.

- Covenant of insurance requires the borrower to carry adequate homeowners insurance to protect the lender interest in the collateral in case of the damage or destruction of a part of the property.

- Covenant of good repair requires that the borrower keep the collateral in good condition. This is also sometimes referred to as the covenant of preservation and maintenance.

The lender is also provided with the right to inspect the property to ensure it is being maintained in a manner that protects the value of the collateral given to the lender.

A clause referred to an acceleration clause is frequently incorporated into the mortgage. The acceleration clause permits the lender to demand all monies owed as payable immediately. If the borrower cannot pay the money owed in full, a foreclosure proceeding is implemented and the property is sold with the lender receiving monies from the sale to pay the funds owed. This clause is used if the borrower breaks any clause included in the agreement.

A clause referred to as an alienation clause or due-on-sale clause is frequently incorporated into the mortgage. This allows the lender to call the entire loan balance as due if the property is sold or conveyed by the borrower to another individual.

If any part of all of the property is taken by the act of eminent domain this clause provides the lender with the right to receive any money paid as part of the action to offset the balance of the loan owed.

The borrower acknowledges the mortgage by the signing of the document. In some states, an authorized person such as a notary public or an officer of the court must witness this signature.

When a note or loan is paid in full, the lender will typically return the promissory note to the borrower. The lender will also provide the borrower with a satisfaction of mortgage document that states the promissory note has been paid in full. This allows the mortgage to be discharged from the public records. It is important that this document be recorded by the public recorder in the same county in which the original mortgage document was recorded.

SETTLEMENT STATEMENT

The settlement statement also called the HUD 1 or closing statement itemizes all of the closing costs payable at the closing or settlement meeting and details the financial negotiations of the transaction. The settlement statement provides a detailed overview of how all of the funds pertinent to the transaction are being applied.

The settlement statement created at the time the initial note was finalized will contain information regarding the borrower's actual investment in the property and specifics regarding the details of the transaction as reported by a third party. The obtainment of the settlement statement provides the Investor with a third party verification that the transaction occurred as reported by the seller of the note.

It is important that you understand the components of the settlement statement as these documents will appear not only during the screening of notes, but at any closing where a note secured by real property is being transferred from the seller to the investor. The review of a settlement statement in relationship to a note transfer that you have negotiated is critical to ensuring smooth closings. By gaining a comprehensive understanding of the elements of the settlement statement, you will obtain the skills necessary to review the statement and locate any potential errors in the financials of the closing before the errors become an issue for either the seller or the investor. It is a part of your function to ensure smooth closings and one method that you may employ to ensure these processes flow smoothly is to confirm that the inclusions of the settlement statement match the transactions specifics that you have negotiated.

The settlement statement is the statement that itemizes all closing costs payable at the closing or settlement meeting. The borrower and seller portions of the settlement statement will breakdown all expenses and receipts on each party's behalf. The settlement statements should mirror the terms agreed upon during the contract negotiations and stipulated on the note agreement. Included in the seller's portion will be any liens or mortgages that must be paid to secure a clear title to the property, any seller concession toward the buyer's closing costs (as negotiated in the Sales Agreement) and any additional charges for which the seller is responsible.

Page one section 100 will contain the total of all costs involved with the actual loan process.

These will include the sales price, settlement charges and any pro-rated taxes due or owed.

The seller's portion of the settlement statement breaks down all items on the seller's behalf. Included in the seller's portion will be:

- Any liens or mortgages that must be paid to secure a clear title to the property

- Any seller concession toward the buyer's closing costs (as negotiated in the Sales Agreement)

- Any additional charges for which the seller is responsible

- Any prorated items the seller has agreed to pay as negotiated in the sales agreement

- Any other costs the seller has incurred that must be paid at the closing table

The settlement statement contains the final figures pertaining to the loan
Page one section 100 will contain the total of all costs involved with the loan process.
These will include

- The sales price

- Settlement charges

- Any pro-rated taxes due from the borrower

Section 200 will contain all amounts, which are paid on behalf of the borrower. These will include

- Any deposit or earnest money the borrower paid at the time of the Sales Agreement negotiation

- Any additional deposits or payments made by the borrower in the course of the loan processing

- The loan amount as negotiated with the lender

- Any assumed loans the borrower is taking

- Any seller financing as negotiated at the time of the sales agreement

- Any closing costs to be paid by the seller as negotiated at the time of the Sales Agreement

- Any additional adjustments that the Title Company has determined must be made to the finances of the package

The figures will be calculated, taking the amount paid on behalf of the borrower (220) and the amount due from the borrower (120) to determine the exact figure the borrower is required to bring to the closing table.

Page two of the settlement statement contains a more detailed breakdown of the charges included in the section titled settlement charges to borrower. The fees and costs being charges on the loan will be included in this section. These figures will mirror the good faith estimate making an error relatively simple to find.

F. Type of Loan			
1__ FHA 2__ FmHA 3__ Conv 4__ VA 5__ Conv Ins	6. File Number:	7. Loan Number:	8. Mortgage Insurance Case Number

G.Note: This form is furnished to give you a statement of actual settlement costs. Amounts paid to and by the settlement agent are shown. Items marked "(P&C)" were paid outside the closing; they are shown here for informational purposes and are not included in the totals.

D. Name & Address of Borrower.	E. Name & Address of Seller	F. Name & Address of Lender
G. Property Location	H. Settlement Agent Place of Settlement:	I. Settlement Date

J. Summary of Borrower's Transaction		K. Summary of Seller's Transaction	
100. Gross Amount Due From Borrower		**400. Gross Amount Due To Seller**	
101. Contract Sales Price		401. Contact Sales Price	
102. Personal Property		402. Personal Property	
103. Settlement Charges to borrower (line 1400)		403.	
104.		404.	
105.		405.	
Adjustments for items paid by seller in advance		Adjustments for items paid by seller in advance	
106. City / Town Taxes for		406. City / Town Taxes for	
107. County Taxes for		407. County Taxes for	
108. Assessments for		408. Assessments for	
109.		409.	
110.		410.	
111.		411.	
112.		412.	
120. Gross Amount Due From Borrower		**420. Gross Amount Due To Seller**	
200. Amounts Paid By Or In Behalf Of Borrower		**500. Reductions In Amount Due To Seller**	
201. Deposit or earnest money		501. Excess deposit (see instructions)	
202. Principal amount of new loan(s)		502. Settlement charges to seller (line 1400)	
203. Existing loan(s) take subject to		503. Existing loan(s) taken subject to	
204.		504. Payoff of first mortgage loan	
205.		505. Pay off of second mortgage loan	
206.		506.	
207.		507.	
208.		508.	
209.		509.	
Adjustments for items unpaid by seller		**Adjustments for items unpaid by seller**	
210. City / Town Taxes for		510. City / Town Taxes for	
211. County Taxes for		511. County Taxes for	
212. Assessments for		512. Assessments for	
213.		513.	
214.		514.	
215.		515.	
216.		516.	
217.		517.	
218.		518.	
219.		519.	
220. Total Paid By/For Borrower		**520. Total Reduction Amount Due Seller**	
300. Cash At Settlement From/To Borrower		**600. Cash at Settlement To/From Seller**	
301. Gross amount due from borrower (line 120)		601. Gross amount due to seller (line 420)	
302. Less amounts paid by/for borrower (line 220)	( )	602. Less reductions in amt due seller (line 520)	( )

Figure 6:7 – Sample HUD 1 Settlement Statement – HUD Release

	Paid From Borrowers Funds at Settlement	Paid From Seller's Funds at Settlement
700. Total Sales/Brokers commission based on price $ @ %		
Division of Commission (line 700) as follows:		
701. $ to		
702. $ to		
703 Commission paid at Settlement		
704.		
800. Items Payable in Connection with Loan		
801. Loan Origination Fee %		
802. Loan Discount %		
803. Appraisal Fee to		
804. Credit Report to		
805. Lender's Inspection Fee		
806. Mortgage Insurance Application Fee to		
807. Assumption Fee		
808.		
809.		
810.		
900. Items Required By Lender To Be Paid In Advance		
901. Interest from to @$ / day		
902. Mortgage Insurance Premium for months to		
903. Hazard Insurance Premium for years to		
904.		
905.		
1000. Reserves Deposited With Lender		
1001. Hazard Insurance months @$ per month		
1002. Mortgage Insurance months @$ per month		
1003. City Property Taxes months @$ per month		
1004. County Property Taxes months @$ per month		
1005. Annual Assessments months @$ per month		
1006. months @$ per month		
1007. months @$ per month		
1008. months @$ per month		
1100. Title Charges		
1101. Settlement or closing fee to		
1102. Abstract or title search to		
1103. Title examination to		
1104. Title insurance binder to		
1105. Document preparation to		
1106. Notary fees to		
1107. Attorney's fees to		
(includes above items numbers:)		
1108. Title Insurance to		
(includes above items numbers:)		
1109. Lender's coverage $		
1110. Owner's coverage $		
1111.		
1112.		
1200. Government Recording and Transfer Charges		
1201. Recording fees: Deed $: Mortgage $: Releases $		
1202. City/county tax/stamps: Deed $: Mortgage $		
1203. State tax/stamps: Deed $: Mortgage $		
1204.		
1205.		
1300. Additional Settlement Charges		
1301. Survey to		
1302. Pest Inspection to		
1303.		
1304.		
1305.		
1400. Total Settlement Charges (enter on lines 103, Section J and 502, Section K)		

Figure 6:8 – Sample HUD 1 Settlement Statement – HUD Release

101 – 401	The sales price	Included in these sections will be the exact figure the buyer is paying and the seller is receiving for the property
103	Total Buyer's Settlement Charges	The total of all settlement charges included on page 2 of the form will be calculated and entered.
109 – 112	Pro-rata	The pro-rata calculations of the hazard insurance premium, utility charges or other recurring bills that are to be divided, if applicable, is entered into this section.
120	Gross Amount	The gross amount due from the buyer is tallied and entered
201	Earnest Money	The buyer is credited with the earnest money deposit made during the negotiation of the sales agreement and any additional deposits made throughout the period between the sales agreement negotiation and the closing of the loan.

L. SETTLEMENT CHARGES

700	TOTAL SALES/BROKER'S COMMISSION based on price $ @ %= PAID FROM BORROWER'S FUNDS AT SETTLEMENT PAID FROM SELLER'S FUNDS AT SETTLEMENT
701	Division of the commission
702	Division of the commission
703	Commission paid at Settlement
704.	
800	Items Payable in Connection with Loan:
	These are the fees that lenders charge to process, approve and make the mortgage loan
801	Loan Origination
	This fee is usually known as a loan origination fee but

sometimes is called a "point" or "points." It is paid to the lender.

802	Loan Discount	Also often called "points" or "discount points," a loan discount is a one-time charge imposed by the lender or broker to lower the rate at which the lender or broker would otherwise offer the loan.
803	Appraisal Fee	This charge pays for an appraisal report made by an appraiser.
805	Credit Report Fee	This fee covers the cost of a credit report.
806	Lender's Inspection Fee	This charge covers inspections, often of newly constructed housing, made by employees of the lender or by an outside inspector. Pest or other inspections made by companies other than the lender are discussed in line 1302.
807	Mortgage Insurance Application Fee	This fee covers the processing of an application for mortgage insurance.
808	Assumption Fee	This is a fee, which is charged when a buyer "assumes" or takes over the duty to pay the seller's existing mortgage loan.
809	Mortgage Broker Fee	Fees paid to mortgage brokers would be listed here.
900	Items Required by Lender to Be Paid in Advance:	Certain items may require payment at the time of settlement, such as accrued interest, mortgage insurance premiums and hazard insurance premiums.
901	Interest	The interest that accrues from the date of settlement to the first monthly payment.
902	Mortgage Insurance Premium	The first years mortgage insurance premium or a lump

sum up-front premium.

903	Hazard Insurance Premium	Hazard insurance protects against loss due to fire, windstorm, and natural hazards.

Investors or lenders often require the borrower to bring to the settlement a paid-up first year's policy   or to pay for the first year's premium at settlement.

904	Flood Insurance	If the property requires flood insurance, the premium is usually listed here.

1000	RESERVES DEPOSITED WITH LENDER:	These lines identify the payment of taxes and/or insurance and other items that must be made at settlement to set up an escrow account.

1001 Hazard Insurance   months @ $ per month

1002 Mortgage insurance   months @ $ per month

1003. City property taxes   months @ $ per month

1004 County property taxes   months @ $ per month

1005 Annual assessments   months @ $ per month

1006   months @ $ per month

1007   months @ $ per month

1008 Aggregate Adjustment

1100	Title Charges:	Title charges may cover a variety of services performed by title companies and others.

1101 Settlement or Closing Fee This fee is paid to the settlement agent or escrow holder.

Responsibility for payment of this fee should negotiated between the seller and the buyer.

1102 Abstract of Title/
Title Examination/ Binder — The charges on these lines cover the costs of the title search and examination.

1105 Document Preparation — This is a separate charged to cover the costs of preparation of final legal papers, such as a mortgage, deed of trust, note or deed.

1106 Notary Fee — This fee is charged for the cost of having a person witness the signing of the documents.

The costs associated with this entry will be those associated with gaining your services as the settlement agent.

1107 Attorney's Fees — The cost of any attorney appears here.

1108 Title Insurance — The total cost of owner's and lender's title insurance is shown here.

1109 Lender's Title
Insurance — The cost of the lender's policy is shown here.

1115 Owner's (Buyer's)
Title Insurance: — The cost of the owner's policy is shown here.

1200 Government Recording
Transfer Charges: — Transfer taxes, which in some localities are collected whenever property changes hands or a mortgage loan is made, are set by state and/or local governments.

City, county and/or state tax stamps may have to be purchased as well (lines 1202 and 1203).

1201	Recording fees	Deed $; Mortgage $; Releases $
1202	City/county tax/ stamps	Deed $; Mortgage $
1203	State tax/stamps	Deed $; Mortgage $
1204		
1205		
1301	Additional Settlement Charges:	
1302	Survey	If it is required that a surveyor conduct a property survey the cost is entered here.
1303	Pest and Other Inspections	This fee is to cover inspections for termites or other pest infestation.
1304	Lead-Based Paint Inspections	This fee is to cover inspections or evaluations for lead-based paint hazard risk assessments and may be on any blank line in the 1300 series.

1400   Total Settlement Charges:

- The sum of all fees in the borrower's column entitled "Paid from Borrower's Funds at Settlement" is placed here.
  This figure is then transferred to line 103 of Section J, "Settlement charges to borrower" in the Summary of the Borrower's Transaction on page 1 of the HUD-1 Settlement Statement. The settlement charges will then be added to the purchase price.

- The sum of all of the settlement fees paid by the seller is transferred to line 502 of Section K, Summary of Seller's Transaction on page 1 of the HUD-1 Settlement Statement.

- Paid Outside Of Closing ("POC") Some fees may be listed on the HUD-1 to the left of the borrower's column and marked "P.O.C." Fees such as those for credit reports and appraisals are usually paid by the borrower before closing/ settlement.

- The first page of the HUD-1 Settlement Statement summarizes all the costs and adjustments for the borrower and seller.

  Section J is the summary of the borrower's transaction.

  Section K is the summary of the seller's side of the transaction.

  Section 100 summarizes the borrower's costs, such as the contract cost of the house, any personal property being purchased, and the total settlement charges owed by the borrower from Section L.

  Beginning at line 106, adjustments are made for items (such as taxes, assessments, and fuel) that the seller has previously paid and for which the borrower will reimburse the seller.
  All financial matters pertinent to the transaction will be included on the settlement statement. All parties will sign the statement to confirm that they understand and agree with the inclusions.

APPRAISALS

Appraisals are another vital area in which you must obtain knowledge. Many of the documentation items we have discussed relate to the borrower and their situation. An essential factor to the Investor is the value and condition of the property that secures the note.

- The borrower is responsible for repaying the loan.

- The property acts as collateral, in the event the borrower does not fulfill their obligations.

The Investor will thoroughly scrutinize property appraisals and other information. An effective Note Broker will understand the appraisal process, the components of an appraisal and areas within the appraisal that present red flags to Investors.

- A Red flag is any information that appears regarding issues that will stand in the way of the completion of the note transfer.

Appraisers are critical to a variety of components of the lending process. The valuation and accuracy of an appraisal must be dependable. Appraisals will be used for

- Sales Price Negotiation
- Loan-to-Value Assessment
- Collateral Security
- Homeowner's Insurance Policies
- Title Insurance Policies
- Borrower Equity
- Determining necessary repairs to the property
- Equity assessment
- Note discount determination

Kenney

UNIFORM RESIDENTIAL APPRAISAL REPORT

The purpose of this summary appraisal report is to provide with an accurate, and adequately supported opinion of market value of the subject property			
Property Address	City	State	Zip Code
Borrower	Owner of Public Record	County	
Legal Description			
Assessor's Parcel #	Tax Year	R.E. Taxes $	
Neighborhood Name	Map Reference	Census Tract	
Occupant __ Owner __ Tenant __ Vacant	Special Assessments $	__ PUD HOA $ __ per year __ per month	
Property Rights Appraised __ Fee Simple __ Leasehold __ Other (describe)			
Assignment Type __ Purchase Transaction __ Refinance Transaction __ Other (describe)			
Lender Client	Address		
Is the subject property currently offered for sale or has it been offered for sale in the twelve months prior to the effective date of this appraisal __ yes __ no			
Report data source(s) used offering prices(s), and date(s)			
I __ did __ did not analyze the contract for sale for the subject purchase transaction. Explain the results of the analysis of the contract for sale or why analysis was not performed.			
Contract Price $ Date of Contract Is the property seller the owner of public record __ Yes __ No Data Source(s)			
Is there any financial assistance (loan charges, sale concessions, gift or down payment assistance, etc.) to be paid by any party on behalf of the borrower? __ Yes __ No If yes, report the total dollar amount and describe the items to be paid.			

Note: Race and racial composition of the neighborhood are not appraisal factors

Neighborhood Characteristics			One-Unit Housing Trends				One-Unit Housing		Present Land Use %		
Location	Urban	Suburban	Rural	Property Values	Increasing	Stable	Declining	PRICE	AGE	One-Unit	%
Built-Up	Over 75%	25-75%	Under 25%	Demand Supply	Shortage	In Balance	Over Supply	$ (000)	(yrs)	2-4 Unit	%
Growth	Rapid	Stable	Slow	Marketing Time	Under 2 mth	3-6 mths	Over 6 mths	Low		Multi-Family	%
Neighborhood Boundaries								High		Commercial	%
								Pred.		Other	%

Neighborhood Description

Market Conditions (including support for the above conclusions)

Dimension	Area	Shape	View
Specific Zoning Classification	Zoning Description		
Zoning Compliance __ Legal __ Legal Nonconforming (Grandfathered use) __ No Zoning __ Illegal (describe)			
Is the highest and best use of the subject property as improved (or as proposed per plans and specifications) the present use? __ Yes __ No If No, describe			

Utilities	Public Other (describe)	Public Other (describe)	Off-site Improvements – Type Public Private
Electricity		Water	Street
Gas		Sanitary Sewer	Alley
FEMA Special Hazard Area __ Yes __ No FEMAL Flood Zone		Fema Map #	FEMA Map Date
Are the utilities and off-site improvements typical for the market area __ Yes __ No If No, describe			
Are there any adverse site conditions or extreme factors (easements, encroachments, environmental conditions and uses, etc.)? __ Yes __ No If Yes, describe			

General Description		Foundation		Exterior Description materials/condition		Interior	materials/condition
Units One	One w Accessory Unit	__ Concrete Slab __ Crawl Space		Foundation Walls		Floors	
# of Stories		__ Full Basement __ Partial Basement		Exterior Walls		Walls	
Type Det Att S-Dec / End Unit		Basement Area	sq ft	Roof Surface		Trim/Finish	
__ Existing __ Proposed __ Under Cons		Basement Finish	%	Gutters & Downspouts		Bath Floor	
Design (Style)		__ Outside Entry/ Exist __ Sump Pump		Window Type		Bath Wainscot	
Year Built		Evidence of __ Infestation		Storm Sash / Insulated		Car Storage None	
Effective Age (Yrs)		__ Dampness __ Settlement		Screens		__ Driveway # of Cars	
Attic	None	Heating FWA HWBB Radiant		Amenities	Woodstove(s)	Driveway Surface	
__ Drop Stair __ Stairs		__ Other __ Fuel		Fireplaces #	Fence	__ Garage # of Cars	
__ Floor __ Scuttle		Cooling Central Air Conditioning		Patio/Deck	Porch	__ Carport # of Cars	
__ Finished __ Heated		__ Individual __ Other		Pool	Other	__ Att __ Det __ Built-in	
Appliances Refrigerator Range/Oven Dishwasher Disposal Microwave Washer/Dryer Other (describe)							
Finished area above grade contains:		Rooms	Bedrooms	Bath(s)	Square Feet of Gross Living Area Above Grade		
Additional Features (special energy efficient items, etc.)							

Describe the conditions of the property (including needed repairs, deterioration, renovations, remodeling, etc.)

Are there any physical deficiencies or adverse conditions that affect the livability, soundness, or structural integrity of the property? __ Yes __ No If Yes, describe

Figure 6:9 – Sample Uniform Residential Appraisal Report Page 1 – HUD Release

UNIFORM RESIDENTIAL APPRAISAL REPORT

There are	comparable properties currently offered for sale in the subject neighborhood ranging in price from $	to $
There are	comparable sales in the subject neighborhood within the past twelve months ranging in sales price from $	to $

FEATURE	SUBJECT	COMPARABLE SALE #1	COMPARABLE SALE #2	COMPARABLE SALE #3
Address				
Proximity to Subject				
Sale Price	$	$	$	$
Sale Price/Gross Liv Area	$　　　sq ft	$　　　sq ft	$　　　sq ft	$　　　sq ft
Data Source(s)				
Verification Source(s)				

VALUE ADJUSTMENTS	DESCRIPTION	DESCRIPTION	Adjustment	DESCRIPTION	Adjustment	DESCRIPTION	Adjustment
Sales or Financing Concessions							
Date of Sale / Time							
Location							
Leasehold/Fee Simple							
Site							
View							
Design (Style)							
Quality of Construction							
Actual Age							
Condition							
Above Grade Room Count	Total　Bdrms　Baths	Total　Bedrms　Baths		Total　Brms　Baths		Total　Brms　Baths	
Gross Living Area	sq ft	sq ft		sq ft		sq ft	
Basement & Finished Rooms Below Grade							
Functional Utility							
Heating / Cooling							
Energy Efficient							
Garage / Carport							
Porch/Patio/Deck							
Net Adjustment		+ 　 -	$	+ 　 -	$	+ 　 -	$
Adjusted Sales Price of Comps		Net Adj　　%　Gross Adj　　%	$	Net Adj　　%　Gross Adj　　%	$	Net Adj　　%　Gross Adj　　%	$

I __ did __ did not research the sale or transfer history of the subject property and comparable sales. If not, explain

My research __ did __ did not reveal any prior sales or transfers of the subject property for the three years prior to the effective date of this appraisal.

Data source(s)

My research __ did __ did not reveal any prior sales or transfers of the comparables sales for the year prior to the date of sale of the comparable sale.

Data source(s)

Report the results of the research and analysis of the prior sale or transfer history of the subject property and comparable sales (report additional on pg 3)

ITEM	SUBJECT	COMPARABLE SALE #1	COMPARABLE SALE #2	COMPARABLE SALE #3
Date of Prior Sale/Transfer				
Price of Prior Sale/Transfer				
Data Source(s)				
Effective Date of Data Source(s)				

Analysis of prior sale or transfer history of the subject property and comparable sales

Summary of Sales Comparison Approach

Indicated Value by Sales Comparison Approach $

Indicated Value by: Sales Comparison Approach $　　　　Cost Approach (if developed) $　　　　Income Approach (if developed)$

The appraisal is made __ as is __ subject to completion per plans and specifications on the basis of a hypothetical condition that the improvements have been completed. __ subject to the following repairs or alterations on the basis of a hypothetical condition that repairs have been completed, or __ subject to the following required inspection based on the extraordinary assumption that the condition or deficiency does not require alteration or repair.

Figure 6:16 – Sample Uniform Residential Appraisal Report Page 2 – HUD Release

Subject

The purpose of this summary appraisal report is to provide with an accurate, and adequately supported opinion of market value of the subject property			
Property Address	City	State	Zip Code
Borrower	Owner of Public Record	County	
Legal Description			
Assessor's Parcel #	Tax Year	R.E. Taxes $	
Neighborhood Name	Map Reference	Census Tract	
Occupant __ Owner __ Tenant __ Vacant	Special Assessments $	__ PUD HOA $	__ per year __ per month

Figure 6:10 – Uniform Residential Appraisal Report Extraction – HUD Release

The first section of the URAR is the section that pertains to the general details of the property being assessed and the individuals involved in the transaction.

- Property Address

- Borrower Name

- Owner of Public Record

- Legal Description

- Assessor's Parcel Number

    Tax Year
    Real Estate Tax Amount

- Neighborhood Name

    Map Reference
    Census Tract

- Occupancy of the Property

    Owner
    Tenant
    Vacant

- Special Assessments

    PUD
    HOA
    Terms

- Property Rights Appraised

    Fee Simple
    Leasehold
    Other

- Assignment Type

    Purchase Transaction
    Refinance Transaction
    Other

- Data Source Information

The note broker should confirm that the information included in these sections match the information submitted on the note and other package components.

You should scrutinize any variances between the documents to determine which document contains the error.

The individual responsible for the document should address the error in writing.

CONTRACT

I __ did __ did not analyze the contract for sale for the subject purchase transaction. Explain the results of the analysis of the contract for sale or why analysis was not performed.		
Contract Price $ Date of Contract	Is the property seller the owner of public record __ Yes __ No Data Source(s)	
Is there any financial assistance (loan charges, sale concessions, gift or down payment assistance, etc.) to be paid by any party on behalf of the borrower? __ Yes __ No If yes, report the total dollar amount and describe the items to be paid.		

Figure 6:11 – Uniform Residential Appraisal Report Extraction – HUD Release

Data pertaining to any sales contract or other contract that is a part of the transaction will be included within this section. You will wish to supply a copy of the contract to the appraiser at the time of the appraisal request.

Upon receipt of the completed appraisal, you should review the inclusions within the section to confirm that they match the details of the transaction you used to structure the note package.

CONTRACT REVIEW

The appraiser will note whether the details of the contract were/were not reviewed during the completion of the appraisal process.

- Contract Price

- Date of Contract

- Confirmation of Seller Financial Assistance

Neighborhood

Note: Race and racial composition of the neighborhood are not appraisal factors			
Neighborhood Characteristics	One-Unit Housing Trends	One-Unit Housing	Present Land Use %
Location __ Urban ___ Suburban __ Rural	Property Values __ Increasing ___ Stable ___Declining	PRICE AGE	One-Unit %
Built-Up __ Over 75% __ 25-75% ___ Under 25%	Demand Supply __ Shortage ___ In Balance __ Over Supply	$ (000) (yrs)	2-4 Unit %
Growth ___ Rapid ___ Stable ___ Slow	Marketing Time __ Under 2 mth __ 3-6 mths ___ Over 6 mths	Low	Multi-Family %
Neighborhood Boundaries		High	Commercial %
		Pred.	Other %
Neighborhood Description			

Figure 6:12– Uniform Residential Appraisal Report Extraction – HUD Release

Neighborhood Information

This section contains information concerning neighborhood information.

Each section must be completed. There should be no blank lines or unchecked boxes.

If there are blank places in the neighborhood section or the information contained does not agree with other property documentation that the seller has provided for you, you should have the individual responsible for the error correct the omission or error.

Neighborhood Red Flags

Assessments within the neighborhood section present vital information that may effect the value of the property and therefore the note investors security in the property.

Any variance from a positive answer or an uncommon answer should be scrutinized. The note broker should discuss these variances with the Appraiser to determine if the information is correct.

Market Characteristics and Conditions

Neighborhood Description
Market Conditions (including support for the above conclusions)

Figure 6:13 – Uniform Residential Appraisal Report Extraction – HUD Release

This section may generate Red Flags.

The note broker should carefully review the appraiser's comments. Any comment that could be considered a negative factor should be addressed before submitting the appraisal to the note investor.

SITE

Dimension	Area	Shape	View
Specific Zoning Classification	Zoning Description		
Zoning Compliance __ Legal __ Legal Nonconforming (Grandfathered use) __ No Zoning __ Illegal (describe)			
Is the highest and best use of the subject property as improved (or as proposed per plans and specifications) the present use? __ Yes __ No If No, describe			
Utilities Public Other (describe)	Public Other (describe)	Off-site Improvements – Type Public Private	
Electricity __ __	Water __ __	Street __ __	
Gas __ __	Sanitary Sewer __ __	Alley __ __	
FEMA Special Hazard Area __ Yes __ No FEMAL Flood Zone	Fema Map #	FEMA Map Date	
Are the utilities and off-site improvements typical for the market area __ Yes __ No If No, describe			
Are there any adverse site conditions or extreme factors (easements, encroachments, environmental conditions and uses, etc.)? __ Yes __ No If Yes, describe			

Figure 6:14 – Uniform Residential Appraisal Report Extraction – HUD Release

The site segment of the appraisal describes the parcel on which the subject property is built and any issue regarding site usage that are apparent.

Any issues with the use of the land or easements, encroachment or other factors affecting the land should be reviewed and addressed. Issues affecting the use of the land may need to be corrected before the closing of the loan. Investor guidelines will dictate what generates a red flag stipulation regarding site and site usage.

You should carefully review the investor's guidelines as applied to the site of a property.

Improvements

General Description	Foundation	Exterior Description materials/condition	Interior	materials/condition
Units __ One __ One w Accessory Unit	__ Concrete Slab __ Crawl Space	Foundation Walls	Floors	
# of Stories	__ Full Basement __ Partial Basement	Exterior Walls	Walls	
Type __ Det __ Att __ S-Dec / End Unit	Basement Area sq ft	Roof Surface	Trim/Finish	
__ Existing __ Proposed __ Under Cons	Basement Finish %	Gutters & Downspouts	Bath Floor	
Design (Style)	__ Outside Entry/ Exist __ Sump Pump	Window Type	Bath Wainscot	
Year Built	Evidence of __ Infestation	Storm Sash / Insulated	Car Storage _____ None	
Effective Age (Yrs)	__ Dampness __ Settlement	Screens	__ Driveway # of Cars	
Attic _____ None	Heating __ FWA __ HWBB __ Radiant	Amenities _____ Woodstove(s)	Driveway Surface	
__ Drop Stair _____ Stairs	__ Other _____ Fuel	__ Fireplaces # _____ Fence	__ Garage # of Cars	
__ Floor _____ Scuttle	Cooling __ Central Air Conditioning	__ Patio/Deck _____ Porch	__ Carport # of Cars	
__ Finished _____ Heated	__ Individual _____ Other	__ Pool _____ Other	__ Att __ Det __ Built-in	
Appliances __ Refrigerator __ Range/Oven __ Dishwasher __ Disposal __ Microwave __ Washer/Dryer __ Other (describe)				
Finished area above grade contains: Rooms Bedrooms Bath(s) Square Feet of Gross Living Area Above Grade				
Additional Features (special energy efficient items, etc.)				
Describe the conditions of the property (including needed repairs, deterioration, renovations, remodeling, etc.)				
Are there any physical deficiencies or adverse conditions that affect the livability, soundness, or structural integrity of the property? __ Yes __ No If Yes, describe				

Figure 6:15 – Uniform Residential Appraisal Report Extraction – HUD Release

Description   Many of the red flags that occur with an appraisal review will occur in this area of the appraisal. All portions of the property should obtain a level of at least an average rating.

If the property rating is less than average, the seller and the buyer will need to determine the steps that will be taken to improve the rating of the property.

The property securing the note is the surety for the investor that they will gain their investment capital back if the borrower defaults on the note. If the condition of the property indicates that the value of the note is not secure, the investor may discount the note offer in order to retain their security.

Comments   The last sections of page one of the URAR will include additional comments from the appraiser.

The note broker should take care to read these comments and those on page three titled Additional Comments.

Appraisers are often aware of items on the URAR that will generate additional property scrutiny by the investor.

The appraiser will typically attempt to address these items within the comment section of the appraisal.

If an error is found on the appraisal or a red flag is noted by the note broker, it is permissible to request the Appraiser address these issues in the comment sections.

The note broker should make this request before submitting the appraisal to the investor whenever possible. This assists in making the investor review process smoother because the investor by having all of the correct information available at the initial review.

We recommend contacting your appraiser if you note a discrepancy, error, or issue on the appraisal report. This recommendation does not indicate that you should influence the appraiser's decision and comments in any manner.

The purpose of the contact is to confirm the information in the URAR is correct according to the appraiser's record.

The only alterations you should request to a completed appraisal are alterations arising because of an error or omission.

You should never attempt to influence or alter the opinion of the appraiser.

VALUATION – SALES COMPARISON APPROACH

FEATURE	SUBJECT			COMPARABLE SALE #1				COMPARABLE SALE #2				COMPARABLE SALE #3			
Address															
Proximity to Subject															
Sale Price	$			$				$				$			
Sale Price/Gross Liv Area	$	sq ft		$		sq ft		$		sq ft		$		sq ft	
Data Source(s)															
Verification Source(s)															
VALUE ADJUSTMENTS	DESCRIPTION			DESCRIPTION			Adjustment	DESCRIPTION			Adjustment	DESCRIPTION			Adjustment
Sales or Financing Concessions															
Date of Sale / Time															
Location															
Leasehold/Fee Simple															
Site															
View															
Design (Style)															
Quality of Construction															
Actual Age															
Condition															
Above Grade Room Count	Total	Bdrms	Baths	Total	Bedrms	Baths		Total	Brms	Baths		Total	Brms	Baths	
Gross Living Area	sq ft			sq ft				sq ft				sq ft			
Basement & Finished Rooms Below Grade															
Functional Utility															
Heating / Cooling															
Energy Efficient															
Garage / Carport															
Porch/Patio/Deck															
Net Adjustment				+	-		$	+	-		$	+	-		$
Adjusted Sales Price of Comps				Net Adj % Gross Adj %			$	Net Adj % Gross Adj %			$	Net Adj % Gross Adj %			$

Figure 6:17– Sample Uniform Residential Appraisal Report Page 2 – HUD Release

Page two of the URAR will contain the actual cost analysis the appraiser completed when assessing the value of the property. The cost analysis may take two forms either the Cost Approach or the Sales Comparison Approach.

You will see the sales comparison approach used more frequently within your files than the cost approach.

The sales comparison data assesses the characteristics and condition of the subject property as compared to other, similar properties sold within a given time period.

Some of the factors that are used for comparison purposes include:

Proximity   The distance between the properties being compared effects the value.

The appraiser should locate similar properties sold within a reasonable time that are close in location to the subject property.

Property values vary greatly from one neighborhood to the next. It is important that property comparisons use properties that are located in similarly valued areas.

Sales Price

The sales price of the comparables is the starting basis that will be used to determine the value of your subject property.

The factors listed below sales price will increase or decrease your property value in comparison with other closed sales in the area.

Any area of your property that is lacking as compared to the sold properties used for comparison will result in a decrease as compared to the sales price of the comparable.

Any area of your property that is a positive as compared to the sold properties used for comparison will result in an increase as compared to the sales price of the comparable.

**Sales Price /
Gross Living**

A dollar figure will be determined for the cost per square foot of property.

This figure is determined by dividing the total sales price by the total square foot of each property.

Data Sources

The appraiser will note the source from which they obtained each entry included in the appraisal.

**Comparison
Factors**

The comparison factors that effect the determination of the value of your property against the sales price of the comparables are:

Sale or Financing Concessions   Any concession relating to the transfer of the comparison property will be included as part of the appraisal. These concessions may alter the transaction through an increase in overall value.

Date of Sale   A date that is too far removed (past) will need to be addressed. This is a red flag issue.

All comparison property sales should occur within a reasonable time to ensure the correct market conditions are being addressed in regards to value.

Location   An assessment of average or above is desired.

Any assessment below average will need to be addressed.

This may be a red flag.

Any variance between the property assessment level and the assessment of the comparison property may result in an alteration to value.

Estate Type   A variance in the type of estates between the properties will need to be addressed.

A variance between the estate type of the properties may result in an alteration to the value.

Site Size   The sites should be similar in size. A large variance will need to be addressed.

A variance between the site size of the properties will result in an alteration to the value.

View   The sites should be of similar rating concerning view assessment.

A variance in the assessment of the view level may result in an alteration in the value.
An assessment below average regarding the view of the subject will need to be addressed. This may result in an alteration to the value.

Design / Style   The properties should be of similar design and appeal levels. A variance will need to be addressed.

A variance in the assessment of design and appeal will result in an alteration in value.

If the subject property obtains a below average design and appeal assessment this may be a red flag.

Quality of Construction   The properties should be of similar quality. Any variance in quality levels will need to be addressed.

A variance in the quality of construction will result in an alteration in the value.

An assessment of below average quality of construction in the subject property may result in required repairs or alteration to the property.

This is a red flag.

An assessment of below average may result in an alteration in the value.

Age of Property   The ages of the properties should be similar. Variances in the ages should be addressed.

Room Count Size   The room counts and size of the properties should be similar. Any variance will need to be addressed.

A variation in the room count of the properties will result in an alteration to the value.

Basement   The size and status (finished or unfinished) of the subject property and comparable properties should be similar.

A variance between the properties will result in an alteration in value.

Functional Utility   The functional utility of all properties should be similar. A variance in the functional utility between the properties will result in an alteration in value.

The subject property should obtain an assessment of at least average.

An assessment below average will need to be addressed.

This is a red flag.

The subject property may require alterations to bring the functional utility of the property to at least an average level or the offer may be reduced due to a below average rating.

Heating /Cooling   The heating and cooling systems of the properties will need to be similar.

A variance in the types or inclusion of heating or cooling systems may result in an alteration in value.

Energy Efficient   The properties should be of similar levels of energy efficiency.

A variance in the energy efficiency levels of the properties will result in an alteration in value.

The subject property must obtain a rating of at least average. A rating of below average will need to be addressed.

This may be a red flag.

Some investors may require alterations to the property to obtain an assessment of at least average.

Garage /Carport   The inclusion of a garage or carport should be similar between all properties.

An alteration to this inclusion will result in an alteration in the value.

**Porch /
Patio / Deck**   The inclusion of a porch, patio or deck should be similar between all properties.

An alteration to this inclusion will result in an alteration in the value.

ITEM	SUBJECT	COMPARABLE SALE #1	COMPARABLE SALE #2	COMPARABLE SALE #3
Date of Prior Sale/Transfer				
Price of Prior Sale/Transfer				
Data Source(s)				
Effective Date of Data Source(s)				

Figure 6:18– Sample Uniform Residential Appraisal Report Page 2 – HUD Release

Adjustments and Sales Price

Net Adjustments

The net adjustments section is where the appraiser will add and subtract all of the alterations to the value that occurred because of variances between the subject property and the comparable properties.

Each item that the appraiser assesses for comparison between the properties will be assigned a value.

Any item that was lacking in the subject property but present in the comparison property will result in a reduction from the sales price of the comparable.

Any items that was lacking in the comparable but present in the subject will result in an increase to the sales price of the comparable.

Adjusted sales price The adjustments will then be added to or subtracted from the sales price of the comparable.

The figure that is obtained from these adjustments is the figure the appraiser believes the subject property would have sold for if given the same buyer, the same time, and the same conditions.

This is the comparison approach to property valuation.

Signature

The signature of the appraiser indicates he has completed the appraiser and certifies that the market value of the property has been duly determined per appraiser guidelines.

Research and Comments

Comments   The comment section on this page will often address issues the appraiser encountered that may affect the appraisal.

Review the comments to determine if the appraiser has addressed any additional red flags that may effect your transaction.

Analysis and Indicated Value

The appraiser will then place the value figure he has obtained through comparison and research on the appraisal page.

This is the final appraised value of the property.

PAGE 3 - Additional Comments

The third page of the appraisal has space for comments of the appraiser.

Any issue noted in the first pages of the appraisal should be addressed in this area.

You should review all comments to ensure you have located each potential red flag contained in the appraisal.

You should ensure the appraiser has addressed each issue that you must have addressed.

COST APPROACH TO VALUE

This approach is used to determine value based upon the replacement cost of the subject property. It is not a typical approach to value that will be used for most of the note transactions you will work with; however, the cost approach will provide important data regarding the reproduction or replacement of the subject property if such a result should become necessary.

INCOME APPROACH

The income approach to value will often be used for rental or other income producing property. The income approach uses many of the same data indicators as the core appraisal but adds the factor of income to the final value of the property.

PUD PROJECT INFORMATION

If the transaction is being based upon a PUD, the final section will play a role in the final value determination. You should review this section for any additional red flags that may become apparent if your transaction involves a PUD.

PAGE 4, 5 and 6 REPORT DISCLOSURES

It is important that you become familiar with the disclosure information included within the appraisal report. The following paragraphs should be reviewed.

AMORTIZATION SCHEDULE

An example amortization schedule is included in an earlier Chapter. This amortization scheduled showed you the monthly payments a Seller or seller can expect to receive on a transaction as well as a detailed summary of the way those payments would be applied toward the transaction.

Frequently, events occur that alter the amortization schedule generated at the beginning of the transaction. These could include:

- Payments that the individual did not make on time or as agreed.

- Additional interest accumulated because of missed or late payments.

- Any payment the individual made in excess of the requirements set forth on the agreement.

    Additional payments such as monthly overages or lump sum applications of funds can alter the amortization schedule.

These alterations will depend on the methods used to apply these payments.

- Any variance from the originally negotiated terms of the transaction, either positive or negative, that occurs outside of the parameters of the note will affect the amortization schedule.

The note seller should provide you with a detailed breakdown of each transaction involving payments that has occurred on the note.

From this information, you and the seller should generate a detail specific amortization schedule showing all applied principal and interest accumulations up to the date of the package creation. This newly created amortization schedule will provide an exact financial statement of the status of the note. This exact status break down will provide the Investor with a substantiated face value of the note. The face value of the note, or amount remaining unpaid, is the starting point for the Investors discount calculations.

PROOF OF PAYMENTS

Many Investors will request proof that the payments set forth in the agreements have been made as agreed. This proof will typically need to be provided through a third party reference source.

Mortgage or rental history is often used to project the probability of the borrower continuing to pay the Investor in a timely manner. The theory behind this is that the manner that the borrower paid previous housing obligations reflects the seriousness with which they will approach the future housing payment obligations.

Mortgage histories are frequently included in a credit report.

If the mortgage/rental history is not included in the credit report, it must be verified in another manner.

Many Investors will not accept a simple verification forms from the private party seller in the transaction as these can easily be falsified. In that instance, you will need to acquire alternate documentation:

12 months most recent cancelled rent checks or money orders

Or

12 months bank statements from the borrower showing concurrent withdrawals in the amount of the monthly rental payment.

Or

12 months bank statement from the seller showing concurrent withdrawals in the amount of the monthly rental payment.

Other options may exist. You should determine potential options available for documentation purposes when you initially interview the Note Seller.

Obtaining this documentation assures the Investor that the transaction specifics have occurred as stated.

- The careful review of the proof of payment history can raise the perceived note value in the Investors assessment.

    This occurs only if the payments have been made in a timely manner.

- The review of the proof of payments history can lower the perceived value of the note if the payments have been late and/or a potential future issue is apparent.

Kenney

REQUEST FOR VERIFICATION OF RENT OR MORTGAGE

Privacy Act Notice: This information is to be used by the agency collecting it or its assignees in determining whether you qualify as a prospective mortgagor under its program. It will not be disclosed outside the agency except as required and permitted by law. You do not have to provide this information, but if you do not your application for approval as a prospective mortgagor or borrower may be delayed or rejected. The information requested in this form is authorized by Title 38, USC. Chapter 37 (if VA); by 12 USC, Section 1701 et. Seq (if HUD/FHA); by 42 USC, Section 1452b (if HUD/CPD); and Title 42 USC, 1471 et. Seq., or 7 USC. 1971 et. Deq. (if USDA/FmHA).

Instructions
Lender – Complete items 1 through 8. Have applicant complete item 9. Forward directly to landlord named in item 1.
Landlord Creditor – Please complete Items 10 through 18 and return directly to lender named in item 2.
This form is to be transmitted directly to the lender and is not to be transmitted through the applicant or any other party.

Part I – Request

1. To (Name and address of Landlord Creditor)	2. From (Name and address of Lender)

I certify that this verification has been sent directly to the landlord/creditor and ahs not passed through the hands of the applicant or any other interested party.

2. Signature of Lender	4. Title	4. Date	6. Lender's Number (Optional)

7. Information To Be Verified

Property Address	Account in the Name of __ Mortgage __ Rental __ Land Contract	Account Number

I have applied for a mortgage loan. My signature below authorizes verification of mortgage or rent information.

8. Name and Address of Applicant(s)	9. Signature of Applicant(s) X X

Part II – To Be Completed by the Landlord/Creditor

We have received an application for a loan from the above, to whom we understand you rent or have extended a loan. In addition to the information requested below, please furnish us with any information you might have that will assist us in processing the loan.

__ Rental Account	__ Mortgage Account	__ Land Contract
10. Tenant Rented from _____ to _____ Amount of rent $_____ per _____ Number of late payments _____ Is account satisfactory? __ Yes __ No	11. Date account opened _____ Original contract amount $_____ Current account balance $_____ Monthly Payment (P&I) $_____ Payment with T&I $_____ Is account current? __ Yes __ No Was loan assumed? __ Yes __ No Satisfactory account? __ Yes __ No	12. Interest Rate _____ % __ Fixed __ ARM __ FHA __ VA __ CONV __ Other Next pay date _____ No. of late payments _____ No. of late charges _____ Owner of First Mortgage _____

Payment History for the previous 12 months must be provided n order to comply with secondary mortgage market requirements.

13. Additional information which may be of assistance in determination of credit worthiness

14. Signature of Landlord/Creditor Representative	15. Title (please print or type)	Date

17. Please print or type name signed in Item 14

Figure 6:19– Sample Verification of Rent or Mortgage – HUD Release

TITLE INSURANCE

Title insurance is the guarantee of what the buyer is receiving when they purchase a piece of real property. The title insurance policy will provide the investor with the details of the title to the property they are gaining an interest in through the transaction as it appears in public records. From the search, the title insurance company agrees to defend against any defects that might arise. This insurance protects the interest of the investor in that it ensures that no other party may come forward and make a claim against the preppy that may minimize the security or interests of the investor.

OWNER'S POLICY
SCHEDULE B

Owners Policy Number: OP No: Reference No:

Lender's Policy No: LP No.

This Policy does not insure against loss or damage (and the Company will not pay costs, attorneys' fees or expenses) which arise by reason of the following:

Special Exceptions: The mortgage, if any, referred to in Item 4 of Schedule , and the following exceptions:

1.   Rights or claims of parties in possession not shown by the public records.

2.   Easements, or claims of easements, not shown by the public records.

3.   Any lien, or right to a lien, for services, labor, or materials heretofore or hereafter furnished, imposed by law and not shown by public records.

4.   Encroachments, overlaps, boundary line disputes, or other matters which would be disclosed by an accurate survey or inspection of the premises.

5.   Possible additional assessments for taxes for new construction or for any major improvements pursuant to provisions of Acts of Assembly relating thereto, not yet due and payable.

6.   Subject to all matters, notes, conditions, restrictions, easements, setback and building lines shown on map 0200-19-7B recorded in the Recorder of Deeds Office for THIS County.

7.   Subject to public and private rights in and to all roads and alleys, public or private, if any affecting the subject property.

<u>THIS IS THE END OF SCHEDULE B</u>

Figure 6:20 Sample Form – Title Insurance Schedule B

PRE-QUALIFICATION

Specific factors have been proven to affect the borrower's probability of default in note transactions. Whenever possible the Investor will wish to assess the credit worthiness of the buyer before purchasing the note.

The discount incorporated into the cash out offer may need to be adjusted in an effort to offset the Investors risk if the credit worthiness of the buyer indicates a higher level of potential risk of default.

The note is only valuable to the Investor if the payments stipulated in the note are made as agreed.

It is important for both potential sellers and potential buyers to understand the aspects of a borrower's profile that can affect the probability of a borrower to repay a loan.

These aspects include items such as:

- Past credit history

- Debt load in relationship to income.

- Employment history

- Other factors as determined by the specific situation of the individual making payments on the note.

The following pages are designed to provide both the note buyer and note seller with information regarding the methods and theories used in the conventional mortgage market to approve or decline a loan. This material is important knowledge when entering into a Note Brokering scenario. It provides a better understanding of the reason buyers desire financing outside of the conventional mortgage arena as well as providing the Investor and Note Broker with knowledge on the proven methods used to assess a potential buyer.

Before beginning to profile a potential note, some basic information will be needed.

The form on the following page is a useful tool for use with both the buyer and the seller.

- It allows the Note Broker to prepare for the negotiation meeting by having all of the preliminary assessment information available.

- The information you will gain using the form also allows you to assess the documentation that may be needed and request it from the seller before the first meeting.

- The form provides the Note Broker with a simplified format that will allow them to obtain all of the information they require for basic profiling of the notes potential in one quick conversation.

Pre-Qualification Questionnaire Date: _____

Referral: _____ Phone: _____

Borrower Name: _____ Co-Borrower Name: _____

Home Phone: _____ Other Phone: _____ Best time(s) to call: _____

DOB: _____ SSN: _____ DOB: _____ SSN: _____

May I run a credit report?___ Yes ___ No   May I run a credit report? ___ Yes ___ No

Employer: _____ Employer: _____

Address: _____ Address: _____

Phone: _____ No yrs. ___ Position: _____ Phone: _____ No yrs. ___ Position: _____

Current Address: _____ Check? ___ Yes ___ No

___ 1st Mortgage ___2nd Mortgage ___ Note Term ___ Note Rate ___ Date of 1st Payment

Gross Income   Debt

Borrowers Mthly	$_____	Mortgage/Rental Payment	$_____
Prev Year	$_____	Auto Payment	$_____
Co-Borrowers Mthly	$_____	Auto Payment #2	$_____
Prev Year	$_____	Installment Debt / Type _____	$_____
Other Income _____	$_____	Installment Debt / Type _____	$_____
Other Income _____	$_____	Other _____	$_____
Total Income	$_____	Total Debt	$_____

DTI _____%

Explanation of Credit Situation/Seller Situation Notes: _____

_____

_____

_____

Outcome:

Figure 7:1 Sample Form – Pre-qualification Questionnaire

Pre-qualification Questionnaire Key

Date

You will always want to date the query.

You may need to 'shelve' a query until an issue has seasoned.

It is our recommendation that you bind each month's questionnaires in a master folder for tracking of referral sources, inquiries vs. applications and other numbers. This information will influence your career.

You will want to keep a copy of any query that does not lead to a full package for follow-up marketing.

Referral

You will want to have referral information available so you may provide follow-up information to the referral source.

Tracking referral source information will allow you to assess your office's marketing and advertising effort effectiveness.

Telephone Number

You will want to have the referral partner's telephone number handy to assist you in maintaining communication.

Look these up yourself, DO **NOT** require the buyer or seller to find the number for you.

Keeping referral partners informed of the progress of a package is one of your greatest assets.

Referral partners appreciate frequent updates. Referral partners are reluctant to work with a note broker that does not consistently provide status information concerning the status of a package.

At some point in the transaction, you will usually need to obtain specifics regarding the actual borrower in the transaction. At times, the Seller will be able to provide you with most of the preliminary information. If you investor requires a full interview with the individual making payment on the note, you will use this form to perform the application interview.

Borrower Name

You will need the full name including middle initial and any additional information Jr., Sr., II

Do not use nicknames.

Note any aliases that the borrower commonly uses.

Names, especially among family, can be very similar.

The more identifying information you can acquire the more pure your credit report will be.

Co-Borrower Name

Some applications will not have a co-borrower.

When a co-borrower exists, it is important to acquire correct identifying information for this person to ensure sufficient pre-qualification data is available.

If the co-borrower information is not readily available at the time of the call, complete the primary borrower information and request the applicant telephone you later the same day with the co-borrower information.

Date of Birth/Social Security Number etc

This information is important for the loan application and vital when you are pulling a credit report.

Always pull credit reports separately.

Even if the borrower and co-borrower are married, you will want to have separate reports.

May I run a credit report?

It is imperative that you obtain permission to pull a borrower's credit report.

Either you or the Seller will have the borrower sign credit-consent forms during the application meeting.

Consent must be available before you may run the report.

You may not run a credit report on any individual without their consent.

Employer

This information aids you and the Investor in determining some of the issues that may arise during the course of the note.

If there is a history of job changes or there is not a 2-year employment history a problem may exist during documentation. Issues such as these are red flags.

Number of years at present employment

You are looking for a minimum of two years employment history.

If the borrower or co-borrower has not been in their current employment two years, you will need to trace back under comments until you acquire a complete two-year history.

Current Address

This is identifying information you will want to have to clarify identity on the credit report.

Number of years at Present address

You will need a two-year residence history for each borrower on the application.

If the borrower has been at the current residence less than two years, you will need to add in comments any additional residence history until you obtain two full years.

This is an excellent reference when you have an application that requires an exception. A common compensating factor is 'at current residence more than 5 years'.

Note Rate

You will verify the note specifics when you review the transaction documentation but gaining the rate applied to the note at the time of the initial transaction will enable you to perform some preliminary profitability calculations.

Note Term

You will verify the note specifics when you review the transaction documentation, but gaining the term applied to the note at the time of the initial transaction will enable you to perform some preliminary profitability calculations.

The term of the note may also indicate possible investors. Investors will have various preferences for their note purchases. Some investors require minimum or maximum terms.

1st Payment

The date of the 1st payment is an important screening question. Many Investors require that a note season for a specific period before they will invest. This allows the Investor to review payment history and other matters prior to investing their capital.

The date of the 1st payment will also allow you to perform some specific preliminary profitability calculations.

Type of Note

1st Mortgage, 2nd Mortgage

The position of the Seller's security in the investment will play a vital role in discount, desirability and security. It is important to understand the type of note you are screening.

You will find some investor offers vary greatly depending on the type of loan.

Income Information

In order to pre-qualify a package you must have complete income information.

Many package refusals occur due to excessive DTI Ratios.

Debt Information

Debt load will be visible on the Credit Report but it is important to ask this information. There may be new debt, which is not yet showing on the report but may crop up before closing the loan.

Child support and alimony payments do affect the debt load.

Explanation of credit situation

This is the opportunity for notes.

The individual making payments on the note will usually explain any information that is present on their credit report.

Gathering this information now allows you to pre-plan the loan package, request any additional documentation that may be needed and is an excellent reference if problems appear later in the loan process.

Outcome

You will want to note what happened with the query.

Some queries will lead to a package remittal. If you process loans for multiple investors, you will want to enter the name of the investor with whom you placed the query.

Always copy the questionnaire and keep one copy for your records.

You will file the queries for follow-up when an issue is resolved.

Note brokering is a service business. The final analysis shows that our most important "product" is our professionalism, attentiveness, and responsiveness to our clients. Much of our communication is on the telephone.

Whether you are communicating with a client, prospect, or others on the telephone or in person, the impression that you convey creates an image in the person's mind. This image will affect your future relationship with that person. For those reasons, it is important that your conversations are controlled and concise. A complete course on telephone and conversational control is available in our advanced program offerings. For now, you must focus on learning career basics.

Chapter

8

CREDIT REPORT

When working in the Note Brokering business it is important that you understand the credit report and the potential impact the information contained on the report may have on the outcome of the transaction. Every action a consumer takes effects their credit report. These actions can have a negative or a positive effect. Credit reports are an overview of a person's entire history of spending and payment habits. Almost everything that we do financially is reported, collected, and stored in each person's credit profile. The primary concern of a Investor is any action that had a negative or derogatory impact on a borrower's credit history.

Debt   The term describing any situation in which funds are borrowed.

Debt Load   The amount of debt an individual is carrying (owes).

                            Debt load may include many items. The most common being:

> Credit card debt
> Department store debt
> Charge accounts
> Auto loans
> Student loans
> Mortgages

                            The ability to borrow more money or to have additional credit extended is effected by how much debt a potential borrower currently carries.

                            As a Note Broker, you will be concerned with debt-to-income ratios.

Debt-to-Income Ratio's The amount of open debt weighed against the borrower's monthly income.

                            The higher the DTI the greater the potential risk of a borrower default on the loan.

                            The credit report will provide a relatively accurate view of the current debt load. The Note Broker should document income for comparison purposes.

Late payments   A late payment is any payment that has been paid more than 30 days past the due date.

                            Late payments can be a severe blemish on the credit report.

                            A late payment will appear on the credit report for two years, though credit bureaus may keep them in the credit file for up to seven years.

Bankruptcy	Bankruptcy can remain on the credit report for as long as 10 years.
Collection accounts	Accounts that a borrower failed to pay as agreed.
	These accounts are turned over to a collection department or agency in the attempt to collect the payments owed. The initial creditor and the collection agencies report these accounts to the bureaus.
	If the borrower has paid these debts in full, have the seller obtain proof from the creditor or a letter and proof from the individual stating that the debt has been completely satisfied and no further action is necessary.
Medical collections	Accounts to medical service providers that the borrower has failed to pay.
	Medical Collection Accounts are often treated differently than other collection accounts.
	You will need to consider the type of collection accounts in the profile.
Credit inquiries	Accesses to a borrower's credit profile.
	These inquiries are visible on the credit report.
	A credit-gathering spree means that the borrower is out to expand their credit quickly for a specific purchase.
	A series of inquiries could also indicate that new credit obligations are present but not visible on the report.
Credit Bureau Scores	Scores generated based solely on credit bureau data.
	Credit Bureau Scores are one of the many elements that are reshaping today's mortgage industry.

Credit scoring has been around since the 1950's and Credit Bureau Scores became widely available in the 1980's.

Credit Scores are now used extensively in such industries as mortgage lending, auto lending and bankcards.

Credit Bureau Score (CBS)

Credit Bureau scoring is a scientific way of assessing how likely a borrower is to pay back a loan.

How is the CBS calculated

A Credit Bureau Score is based on the data available in the borrower's credit report.

The score measures the relative degree of risk a potential borrower represents to the Investor.

A credit bureau score is not a measure of a borrower's income, assets or bank account. These factors are taken into consideration by Investors independent of credit scores.

Score Range

Fair, Isaac Credit Bureau Scores range from approximately 450 to 850 points.

Repositories

Credit scores are available through three national repositories.

The scoring programs of these credit bureaus are called:

BEACON   at EQUIFAX (CBI)
EMPIRICA   at TRANS UNION
TRW/FAIR, ISAAC   at TRW

This score is calculated at the repository and is based on the data within that repositories credit file.

FICO

A Fair, Isaac Credit Bureau Score, sometimes referred to as a FICO score is calculated using a system of scorecards.

In developing these scorecards, Fair, Isaac uses actual credit data from millions of consumers. They apply complex mathematical methods to perform extensive research into credit patterns that forecast credit performance.

Through this process, Fair, Isaac identifies distinctive credit patterns. Each pattern corresponds to a likelihood that a consumer will make his or her loan payments as agreed.

This score is based on all the credit-related data in the credit bureau report – not just negative data such as a missed mortgage payment or bankruptcies.

Score Data

The types of credit information used in the credit bureau scorecards are typically the same items the Investor will use to make a credit decision. These can include:

> Payment history
> Public records and collection items
> Severity, recentness and frequency of delinquencies noted in the trade line section
> Outstanding Debt
> Number of balances recently reported
> Average balance across all trade lines
> Relationship between total balances and total credit limits on revolving trade lines
> Credit History
> Age of oldest trade line
> Inquiries and new account openings
> Number of inquiries in the last year
> Number of new accounts opened in the last year
> Amount of time since most recent inquiry
> Types of credit in use
> Number of trade lines for each type:

>> Bankcard
>> Travel and Entertainment cards
>> Department store cards
>> Personal finance company references
>> Installment loans
>> Other credit

Fair, Isaac observes tens of thousands of credit report histories of mortgage borrowers to determine which credit report items or combination of items are the most predictive of future risk. This data indicates the amount of weight each item should contribute to a credit decision.

FAIR, ISAAC CREDIT BUREAU SCORES DO NOT USE RACE, COLOR, RELIGION, NATIONAL ORIGIN, SEX, MARITAL STATUS, OR AGE AS PREDICTIVE CHARACTERISTICS.

OCCUPATION AND LENGTH OF TIME IN PRESENT HOUSING ARE ALSO NOT USED IN THE SCORECARDS.

ANY INFORMATION THAT IS NOT PRESENT IN THE CREDIT FILE IS NOT USED IN CREATING A CREDIT BUREAU SCORECARD.

Understanding a score's impact

A Fair, Isaac Credit Bureau Score is a means of rank-ordering potential borrowers based on the likelihood that they will pay their credit obligations as agreed.

A higher score indicates a better credit quality. If all other things are equal, borrowers with a score of 640 are less likely to default on a loan than borrowers with a score of 560.

The Fair, Isaac Credit Bureau Score models at each credit repository is of similar design and the scores are scaled to indicate a similar level of risk across all three repositories. In other words, a score of 660 at one bureau will represent a similar level of risk as a score of 660 at another bureau. It is important to note that some reporting agencies may be more regionally applicable than others. Investors will determine which credit-reporting agency is most appropriate for the region in which the borrower is located.

The risk is defined in terms of the number of accounts that remain in good standing compared to those that default.

Credit score ranges for new mortgage borrowers from a national sample

Score Range	Number of good loans for each bad loan showing serious delinquency or foreclosure (# of good to 1 bad)
Below 600	8 to 1
700 – 719	123 to 1
Above 800	1,292 to 1

Credit Bureau Scores will rank-order potential borrowers based on risk or the number of good loans to bad loans denoted by a score. This rank ordering is likely to fluctuate due to changes in the economy, regional differences, changes in product offerings or other reasons.

A Investor using credit scores will compare performance of their investments, by score, over time to determine the relationship of score and performance for their own market environment.

Score Factors – Reason Codes

To understand why a credit report scored the way it did, you must review the reason codes given within each score. These reason codes provide the top reasons why a profile did not score higher. These scores are only the top reasons and other factors probably contribute to the overall score. You should review both the score and the reasons the score ranks where it does.

To find the scores reason code you should locate a number or a letter followed by a brief description.

For example, a score of 540 may have the following factors:

02 – Delinquency on accounts
01 – Amount owed on accounts is too high
09 – Too many accounts opened in the last 12 months
19 – Too few accounts currently paid as agreed

Score factors are less meaningful for higher scoring credit records as they merely point to the reasons why a very good credit report was not perfect.

Examples of adverse factors that may appear on the report as a consideration in the score calculations are

> Current outstanding balances on accounts
> Delinquency report on accounts
> Accounts not paid as agreed
> Too few open accounts
> Too many open accounts
> Too many bank accounts with outstanding balances
> Too many finance company accounts
> Payment history too new to rate
> Number of inquiries within the last 12 months
> Number of accounts opened within the last 12 months
> Balance too high
> Length of credit history
> No recent account information
> Too few accounts rate as current
> Amount past due on accounts
> No adverse factors
> Recent derogatory public record or collection

This is not an all-inclusive listing. The items listed are examples of issues you may find in the score coding section of a report. You should review each report carefully to determine the factors specific to that credit profile.

Increasing the Score

Over time, a borrower can improve the information in his or her credit report by paying credit obligations as agreed and using credit wisely. As derogatory data in the credit report gets older, it affects the score less. A missed payment from four years ago will not count as much as a missed payment from six months ago. As the borrower uses their credit in a more controlled manner, keeping debt load well below their maximum credit limits, their score is also likely to increase.

A credit score, like a credit report, is a snapshot of an individual's changing credit record. If you make a request for a second repository report to get an updated score, the score is likely to change for many reasons. It is not possible to control how that score will change.

The credit items on the report are updated often, so new items are likely to have been added since the previous report. Repeatedly requesting a borrower's credit report may substantially increase the number of inquiries on the repository report, which may affect the score adversely.

Removing Erroneous Information

Consumers who want to address what they believe is erroneous information on a credit report should contact the credit reporting agency which developed the report.

The Fair Credit Reporting Act (FCRA) allows the credit-reporting agency a "reasonable period of time", generally not to exceed 30 days, to investigate consumer disputed items.

A significant number of credit grantors use an automated system for investigating the disputes and respond to the dispute within a few days. Most credit reporting agencies make a special effort to resolve disputed information affecting a mortgage investment decision. The Investor can weigh these factors and documentation provided by the borrower.

Because the score uses all the credit-related data on the credit bureau report and takes into account all contributing factors, removing or changing one specific, derogatory item will not guarantee an increase in Credit Bureau Score. In some cases, a change in the credit bureau report will have little or no effect on the score. Because there are many scorecards using a complex mathematical formula at each of the repositories, it is not possible to estimate how much the score will change if specific derogatory information is removed for a single repository report.

The number of inquiries may or may not be a factor in the score. When inquiries are a factor, they are typically not a strong one.

The law requires a record of all inquiries into the file be kept on file. This means inquiries cannot be removed from the credit report. Consumer disclosure inquiries are not used in determining score. It is up to the Investor, as in all circumstances, to decide what a sufficient credit risk is.

Borrower and Co-Borrower identifying information is entered in this section.
You should verify that all details entered match the information included on the note data sheet

MERGED INFILE CREDIT REPORT			
Prepared For:	Property Address:	Prepared By:	Date Rec:
Attention:	Loan Type: Purpose of Loan: Report Type:	Computer ID: Lender Case #:	Date Comp: Date Revised:

APPLICANT		CO-APPLICANT	
Name: SSN: Marital Status: Home Phone:	DOB: Dependents:	Name: SSN: Marital Status: Home Phone:	DOB: Dependents:
Present Address:		Present Address:	
Since:	Own / Rent	Since:	Own / Rent
Previous Address:		Previous Address:	
From: To:	Own / Rent	From: To:	Own / Rent

The data included in this area may serve as verification data.

This area is not always as up-to-date as the data you will have available directly from the borrower.

Data identifying the types of credit the borrower has available is entered into the report.

Credit payment totals and current balances will appear with the credit summary portion of the report.

This information will enable you to confirm debt ratio information and possible issues that may arise.

CREDIT SUMMARY

	PAYMENTS	BALANCES	LIMITS	TRADES	30+	60+	90+
REVOLVING	0	2061	2200	4	4	4	17
INSTALLMENT	1307	79365	90610	25	34	8	27
REAL ESTATE	378	35384	36600	1	2	0	0
OPEN/OTHER	991	1041	1041	5	0	0	0
TOTAL	2676	117851	129451	38	40	12	44

# INQUIRIES	50	# PUBLIC RECORDS	0	# BANKRUPTCIES	0
WORST TRADE	9	OLDEST DATE	07/01/89	# SATISFACTORIES	17

An analysis of the details of the report will be included within the summary.

2	JUDGEMENT	RPTD – 09/96	VRFD -	OPND –
	CASE – 104		SRCE – 1011	AMT – 13245
	ASSET -	LIAB -	BAL -	LACT – 09/96
			PLTF -	XPN01

This analysis will assist you in completing your Scoring Key as much of the derogatory data you will use during scoring and placement will be summarized here.

1	JUDGEMENT	RPTD – 11/94	VRFD -	OPND –
	CASE – 9401		SRCE – 1016	AMT – 1900
	ASSET -	LIAB -	BAL -	LACT – 01/95
		PLTF -		XPN01

The number of credit inquiries into this profile will be totaled.

The borrower may be required to provide an explanation of excessive inquiries

Specifics regarding public records, bankruptcies and the worst trade you will encounter when grading the report will be included within the credit summary.

The oldest date indicates the first open trade line for the borrower. This will enable you to confirm an adequate credit history is available.

Be certain you confirm the data prior to transfer as some items may be seasoned and therefore not applicable for your purposes

The name of the score included with the report will be included.

Different investors will require the use of specific repository scores. This is a result of regional variations regarding reported matters making one repository more complete than another

The code of the applicable agency will be entered to confirm the source of the score.

EFX = Equifax

8   BEACON SCORE   EFX01
     519
     SERIOUS DELINQUENCY AND DEROGATORY PUBLIC RECORD OR COLLECTION FILED
     AMOUNT OWED ON DELINQUENT ACCOUNTS
     PROPORTION OF BALANCES TO CREDIT LIMITS TOO HIGH ON REVOLVING ACCOUNTS
     LENGTH OF TIME ACCOUNTS HAVE BEEN ESTABLISHED

8   EMPIRICA SCORE   TRU01
     493
     SERIOUS DELINQUENCY, AND PUBLIC RECORD OR COLLECTION FILED
     LEVEL OF DELINQUENCY ON ACCOUNTS
     TIME SINCE DELINQUENCY IS TOO RECENT OR UNKNOWN
     PROPORTION OF REVOLVING BALANCES TO REVOLVING CREDIT LIMITS IS TOO HIGH

8   FAIR ISAAC SCORE   XPN01
     529
     SERIOUS DELINQUENCY AND PUBLIC RECORD OR COLLECTION FILED
     PROPORTION OF BALANCES TOO HIGH ON REVOLVING ACCOUNTS
     NUMBER OF ACCOUNTS DELINQUENT
     LENGTH OF TIME SINCE LEGAL ITEM FILED OR COLLECTION ITEM REPORTED

The factors that affect the score will be included on the report. This information is often referred to by a score factor code.

If a judgment or public record exists in the borrower profile, the details of that record will be included within the report.

This data could include bankruptcy and foreclosure history as well as judgments and other public records.

Any inclusion within this section should be scrutinized thoroughly.

The type of public record will be named.

Dates pertaining to the specific public record will be entered.

This typing will indicate to you the specific handling of the matter per the investor guidelines. Certain types of judgements may affect the property and the note investors offer on the note.

2	JUDGEMENT	RPTD – 09/96	VRFD -	OPND –
	CASE – 104		SRCE – 1011	AMT – 13245
	ASSET -	LIAB -	BAL -	LACT – 09/96
			PLTF -	XPN01

1	JUDGEMENT	RPTD – 11/94	VRFD -	OPND –
	CASE – 9401		SRCE – 1016	AMT – 1900
	ASSET -	LIAB -	BAL -	LACT – 01/95
		PLTF -		XPN01

FRAUD ALERT is becoming an increasingly filled field. Any data that indicates possible fraud activity will be
included within this section

Frequently this information will be generated because of some action by the borrower but all entries should be researched

FRAUD ALERT

1	TRANS ALERT	TRU01
	# INQUIRIES IN LAST 60 DAYS: 04	
	RECORDED INQUIRIES ALTER	
1	HAWK ALERT	TRU 01
	HAWK AVAILABLE AND CLEAR	

Details regarding any activity that may indicate fraud will be included.

AVAILABLE AND CLEAR = No information found

inquiries in the last 60 days = potential credit gathering spree. At times, this could indicate a stolen profile.

The heading section of the CREDIT HISTORY form will provide you with guides to assist in reading the report inclusions.

The history section details each account held by the borrower and is the area you will scrutinize when completing the GRADING KEY.

The name of the creditor and account number will be included on the report

Account numbers are often shortened and the full account number may not appear.

Date Reported is the last reporting date for a particular account.

Not all accounts report on a monthly basis. You may be required to bring the data pertaining to a specific account up-to-date to comply with underwriting requirements

CREDIT HISTORY

E C O A	CREDITOR ACCOUNT NO	DATE RPTED	DATE LAST ACT	DATE OPND	LIMIT / HIGHEST CREDIT	PRESENT STATUS		TERMS	PAY AMT	TYPE AND ACCT STATUS	HISTORICAL STATUS			
						BALANCE OWING	AMOUNT PAST DUE				NO MOS HIIST REV	3 0	6 0	9 0
8	AFM-BLOOM #APRINTLO COLLECTION	02/99	04/94		425	425				OPN05				

Date last active provides you with the last date the account was in use.

Some accounts will be closed and often the history of these accounts will not affect your transaction.

You should review the last active date prior to including an account in your history score.

The opening date of the account allows you to review the historical status with more accuracy.

Date opened may also indicate a current credit-gathering spree that will raise a red flag issue when the report is reviewed by the note investor.

PRESENT STATUS details the current balances and any amounts currently past due for each account.

TERMS AND PAYMENT AMOUNT provide you with details of the account that will effect debt ratios

HISTORICAL STATUS details allow you to review the worst credit history as well as determine when specific credit issues may have occurred.

ECOA	CREDITOR ACCOUNT NO	DATE RPTED	DATE LAST ACT	DATE OPND	LIMIT / HIGHEST CREDIT	PRESENT STATUS		TERMS	PAY AMT	TYPE AND ACCT STATUS	HISTORICAL STATUS			
						BALANCE OWING	AMOUNT PAST DUE				NO MOS HIIST REV	30	60	90
8	AFM-BLOOM #APRINTLO	02/99	04/94		425	425				OPN05				

TYPE AND ACCOUNT STATUS will provide you with the type of account

Ex: Rev = Revolving

And with status information that may effect the inclusion of the account on the history scoring key

Ex: Open = Currently active account

NO MOS HIST REV indicates the number of months detailed within the historical data section.

Investor guidelines will dictate the number of months applicable for grading.

Minimum account history requirements may exist and this area will allow you to assess the ability of the account to meet this requirement.

The numerical entries indicate any late payments to be found within the report. Each account history will contain numbers indicating the status of a particular month's payment.

1 = on time
2 = 30 days late
3 = 60 days late
X = same as previous month

MERGED INFILE CREDIT REPORT

Prepared For:	Property Address:	Prepared By:	Date Rec:
Attention:	Loan Type: Purpose of Loan: Report Type:	Computer ID: Lender Case #:	Date Comp: Date Revised:

APPLICANT

Name:
SSN: DOB:
Marital Status: Dependents:
Home Phone:

Present Address:

Since: Own / Rent

Previous Address:

From: To: Own / Rent

CO-APPLICANT

Name:
SSN: DOB:
Marital Status: Dependents:
Home Phone:

Present Address:

Since: Own / Rent

Previous Address:

From: To: Own / Rent

CREDIT SUMMARY

	PAYMENTS	BALANCES	LIMITS	TRADES	30+	60+
90+						
REVOLVING	0	2061	2200	4	4	4
17						
INSTALLMENT 1307	1307	79365	90610	25	34	8
27						
REAL ESTATE	378	35384	36600	1	2	0
0						
OPEN/OTHER	991	1041	1041	5	0	
0 0						
TOTAL	2676	117851	129451	38	40	
12 44						

INQUIRIES   50   # PUBLIC RECORDS   0   # BANKRUPTCIES   0
WORST TRADE 9   OLDEST DATE 07/01/89   # SATISFACTORIES   17

2	JUDGEMENT	RPTD – 09/96	VRFD -	OPND –
	CASE – 104		SRCE – 1011	AMT – 13245
	ASSET -	LIAB -	BAL -	LACT – 09/96
			PLTF -	XPN01

1	JUDGEMENT	RPTD – 11/94	VRFD -	OPND –
	CASE – 9401		SRCE – 1016	AMT – 1900
	ASSET -	LIAB -	BAL -	LACT – 01/95
		PLTF -		XPN01

CREDIT HISTORY

ECOA	CREDITOR ACCOUNT NO	DATE RPTED	DATE LAST ACT	DATE OPND	LIMIT / HIGHEST CREDIT	PRESENT STATUS		TERMS	PAY AMT	TYPE AND ACCT STATUS	HISTORICAL STATUS			
						BALANCE OWING	AMOUNT PAST DUE				NO MOS HIIST REV	30	60	90
8	AFM-BLOOM #APRINTLO COLLECTIO	02/99	04/94		425	425				OPN05				
											132111111 TRU01			
8	BENEFICL-HFC #7101702	07/00	04/00	03/97	0	0	0	39M 125		INS 01	37	0	0	0
											XX1111111X1111111111X XXX1111111111111111111 TRU01			
8	CAPTIAL 1 BK 05291071382	04/00	01/00	06/96	592	0	0			REV01	41	0	0	0
											111111111111111111111 111111111111111111111 TRU01			
8	CCB 42270972 CREDIT CARD	07/00	02/00	07/98	950	0				REV01	24	0	0	0
											EFX01			
1	CITIBANK 54241800	06/00	06/00	12/99	3500	3516	0	72	72	REV01	8	0	0	0
											11111111 TRU01			
8	CORNER STONE S0000070010	09/00	06/96	09/94	4374	0	0	18M 223		INS00	1	0	0	0
											TRU01			
8	DIRECT MERCH BK 54580000114	07/00	07/00	11/95	2600	2496		83	83	REV01	25	0	0	0
											111111111111111111111 111111111111111111111 XPN01			
8	AFM-BLOOM #APRINTLO COLLEC CLOSED – CONS	02/99	04/94		425	425				OPN05				
											132111111 TRU01			
8	BENEFICL-HFC #7101702 CLOSED	07/00	04/00	03/97	0	0	0	39M 125		INS 01	37	0	0	0
											XX1111111X1111111111X XXX1111111111111111111 TRU01			
8	CAPTIAL 1 BK 05291071382 CLOSED – CONS	04/00	01/00	06/96	592	0	0			REV01	41	0	0	0
											111111111111111111111 111111111111111111111 TRU01			

8	CCB 42270972 CREDIT CARD CREDIT CARD	07/00	02/00	07/98	950	0				REV01	24	0	0	0
											EFX01			
1	CITIBANK 54241800 CREDIT CARD	06/00	06/00	12/99	3500	3516	0	72	72	REV01	8	0	0	0
											11111111 TRU01			
8	CORNER STONE S0000070010 CLOSED AUTO	09/00	06/96	09/94	4374	0	0	18M 223		INS00	1	0	0	0
											TRU01			
8	DIRECT MERCH BK 54580000114 CREDIT CARD	07/00	07/00	11/95	2600	2496		83	83	REV01	25	0	0	0
											11111111111111111111 11111111111111111111 XPN01			
1	FCNB/NEWP 4220507 CHARGE ACCOUNT	07/00	06/00	09/99	900	888		30	30	REV01	10	0	0	0
											11111111111111111111 11111111111111111111 TRU01			
3	FIRST USA BANK NA 5417623 CREDIT CARD	07/00	07/00	12/99	3000	2602	0	65	65	REV01	8	0	0	0
											11111111 TRU01			
2	FNANB 15230035125 CREDIT CARD	09/00	09/00	12/99	3000	1976		79	79	REV01	9	0	0	0
											11111111111111111111 11111 EPN01			
1	FNANB VISA 54063555013	06/00	06/00	06/98	700	0				REV01	27	1	0	0
											X1121111111111111111 EFX01			

Credit History (12 months)
Borrower

Mortgage Last 12 Months	Consumer Last 12 Months	Bankruptcy NOD/Foreclosure	Charge offs/Judgments
_____ X 30	_____ X 30	Chapter _____	# Filed _____
_____ X 60	_____ X 60	Discharge Date:	$ Amount
_____			
_____ X 90	_____ X 90	_____	$ to remain open _____
_____ X 120	_____ X 120	Balances: _____	$ to be paid _____
_____ Level	_____ Level	_____ Level	_____ Credit Score

Estimated Credit Level: _____

Credit History (12 months)
Co-Borrower

Mortgage Last 12 Months	Consumer Last 12 Months	Bankruptcy NOD/Foreclosure	Charge offs/Judgments
_____ X 30	_____ X 30	Chapter _____	# Filed _____
_____ X 60	_____ X 60	Discharge Date:	$ Amount
_____			
_____ X 90	_____ X 90	_____	$ to remain open _____
_____ X 120	_____ X 120	Balances: _____	$ to be paid _____
_____ Level	_____ Level	_____ Level	_____ Credit Score

Estimated Credit Level: _____

Kenney

Credit History Scoring Key

The previous pages have provided you with general information regarding the credit report. You must learn to score a credit report to determine the note program availability for each borrower package. The credit history-scoring key provides a simple method of extracting the necessary information from the report and organizing it for credit grading functions.

To begin review the credit history-scoring key and the sample credit report. Your earlier course work will assist you in locating the information from the report. This key assists you in organizing the information into a format that you can use.

Mortgage History   The first item of importance in the credit report is the mortgage history.

Locate the mortgage for the borrower's primary residence on the report and determine late payments over the last 12 to 24 months. Most investors are interested in only the worst rating.

Example: If the borrower was 1 X 60 days late then the quantity of 30 days late pays is unimportant.

If the borrower does not have a mortgage or rental history on their credit, you will need to acquire the other documentation in order to determine mortgage/rental history levels.

If the borrower has additional real estate beyond their primary residence, you will need to determine if the investor product planned for them counts these as consumer or mortgage debt. A non-residence often rates as consumer debt. You will need to rate the late payments accordingly.

Consumer History   Tally all late payments falling in the consumer debt category.

These may include:

Personal loans
Credit card debt
Revolving lines of credit
Non-residence mortgage loans

Any other reported items that indicate monthly payments

Consumer debt is typically tallied based on the worst piece of history over the last 12-24 months. The exact term depends on the investor guideline criteria.

Bankruptcy/NOD/ Foreclosure

You will need to look under public records as well as the body of the report to determine if any of these items are present.

You will typically become aware to look for these issues during the pre-qualification questionnaire.

Keep in mind that derogatory debt showing on the report and calculated in the first two columns may have been discharged as a part of the Bankruptcy.

If an item is present on the report that was included in Bankruptcy Proceedings, you will need to acquire a credit supplement from the credit-reporting agency verifying this debt as fully discharged.

The Bankruptcy Discharge papers should also contain this information.

Charge Offs / Judgments

Each matrix has different criteria concerning charge offs.

You will need to have an idea of which investor you plan for the submittal of this loan package before determining what is to be paid or remain open.

For the present, you will include ALL charge off/judgment history in the total number and the total balances.

Complete the amount to be paid and the amount to remain open after you determine the investor program you will use.

You may wish to complete credit-scoring forms for each potential investor package until you become familiar with the programs and can determine without the form which programs will be right for each history.

Approval Level   Each piece of the history will denote a level on the chosen product matrix.

Review specific product matrix outlines with your branch manager or within the investor's portfolio to clarify how to rate levels of approval.

A sample matrix and pricing worksheet is included later in the course for practice lessons.

Some programs provide blended levels while some use the lowest level for approvals.

Each investor has a different system for rating approvals and this is information you will need to study in the program guidelines provided by your branch manager or within the investor portfolio.

Credit Score   Each note program has a different method of using credit scores. Some take the middle of the three scores and some are regionally based, as one of the three reporting agencies may be more accurate for your region.

Review your matrix with to clarify how to rate scores for credit grades.

Co-Borrower   The same rating system will apply for the borrower and the co-borrower.

You will need to score the credit reports separately.

Do not count duplicate debt twice.

The credit history form is useful in rating a credit report for quick referral as you review investor matrix in an effort to determine the best products.

Many investors now use a blended matrix when determining the note program that a package may obtain.

A blended program will take the credit score and the borrower's worst piece of credit history and use those factors to determine qualifying programs. Each investor's loan matrix and approval process is different. Regardless of how the investor chooses to rank the programs, you will find it easiest at first to take the information obtained in the credit report and complete the Credit History form.

COMPENSATING CONSIDERATIONS

When the situation of the individual making payments on the note does not meet the expectations the Investor has determined as the most desirable, some other factors may aid the Investor in making a sound decision on the viability of the buyer.

The Investor may choose to purchase the note by considering other factors in the individual's profile. In conventional lending these additional pieces of information are commonly referred to as compensating factors.

It is up to the Note Seller to make as strong a case as possible for the note based on any piece of information that will reflect favorably on the note package from the prospective of the Investor. The following listing includes some items that could be considered compensating factors from the prospective of the Investor. Remember that any item that positively reflects on the situation of the individual making payments, the note or the property securing the note has the potential to be considered a compensating factor by the Investor. The following listing is simply an example listing to provide you and the seller with an idea of the common compensating factors that may be considered.

The borrower's excellent savings ability (as shown by savings accounts, etc)

3 or more months cash reserves

Larger than requested down payment at the time of the note signing

Residual income (excess after expense) of $500 per adult and $250 per child

Time making payments as agreed exceeds 3 years

Time at current employment exceeds 3 years

Overall debt-to-income ratios are lower than the Investor requires

Credit issues can be explained and documented because of an isolated incidence that is unlikely to reoccur

A perfect mortgage history under the note as proven through the credit bureau or other third party documentation

These are only examples of the most commonly used factors. Each situation has a different set of circumstances, it is up to the individual making payments on the note, seller and Note Broker to determine what can be used to create the best possible contract for all parties involved.

DEBT-TO-INCOME RATIO'S

The debt ratio is what will determine "how much" payment a particular individual can afford. The debt ratio is determined by comparing the current amount of money the individual owes with their income to determine how much money is left to spend on a monthly basis.

Following are the two types of debt ratios that are often considered:

Front-End Ratio - this is the gross income divided by the PITI mortgage payment.

In the conventional mortgage marketplace, the standard guideline is 29%. For non-conforming (sub-prime) loan programs, the back-end debt ratio is more often used. This can be as high as 55% depending on the note product being considered.

Back-End Ratio - this is the gross income divided by the PITI mortgage payment and the minimum monthly payments from all other liabilities.

The standard guideline is 41% and the non-conforming guideline can be as high as 55% in the conventional mortgage marketplace. It is important to remember that a higher debt ratio is another common reason an individual will seek creative finance solutions so the Investor may consider higher than average ratios in the notes they purchase.

The Investor will typically review the debt-to-income ratio of the buyer named in the note to determine if the potential risk is manageable. This is another important negotiating factor affecting the note discount figure.

Following are the debts typically used to determine the qualifying ratios:

Front-End Ratios

The current and/or future house payment

Back-End Ratios

The minimum required monthly payments on all of the following:

Auto Loans - (except if there is less than 9 months left to pay off)

Student Loans - (except if there is less than 9 months left to pay off)

Personal Loans (except if there is less than 9 months left to pay off)

Charge Cards - minimum required payments only.

Child Support - (except if there is less than 9 months left to pay off)

Alimony - (except if there is less than 9 months left to pay off)

Federal Tax Lien Repayment Schedules - (if less than 9 months not calculated)

Following are monthly liabilities that are not used to calculate debt ratios:

Utility Bills

Car & Health Insurance

Cell Phone Bills

The percentage of debts to income is called the debt-to-income (a.k.a. back-end) ratio.

An example of the income to debt calculation is as follows:

Income = $3,000

Mortgage Payment = $900

Minimum Monthly Payments = $300

"Mortgage" divided by "Income" = 30%

"Mortgage   +   Monthly Payments" divided by   "Income"   = 40%

In this scenario, the front-end ratio is 30% and the back-end ratio is 40%, which is acceptable for many note investment portfolio guidelines.

All the factors should be taken into account before the note package is offered to the Investor. At times, the Investor may determine a higher discount can offset the risk inherent in a high debt-to-income scenario. At other times, the items already negotiated into the note will be sufficient to offset the Investors perceived risk. One such factor is the interest rate negotiated at the signing of the original note. Many sellers will negotiate a higher interest rate penalty to offset the risk of holding the note on a purchase. The negotiated interest rate may be adequate to compensate the Investor for the increased risk.

Always keep in mind that the higher the interest rates the higher the monthly payment. In situations where the individual making payments has an overall monthly debt at a level that is currently considered excessive, adding interest, which will in turn inflate that monthly debt load, may not be the wisest negotiating point to show the Investor.

DEBT TO INCOME RATIO (DTI%)

Monthly Income

Borrower   Co-Borrower

$_____ Base Pay/ _____ $_____ Base Pay/ _____
$_____ Commission/ _____ $_____ Commission/ _____
$_____ Other _____ $_____ Other _____
$_____ Other _____ $_____ Other _____

$_____ Total Monthly Income $_____ Total Monthly Income

Combined Monthly Income $_____

Monthly Debt

Borrower   Co-Borrower

$_____ House/Rent Payment $_____ House/Rent Payment
$_____ Automobile Payment $_____ Automobile Payment
$_____ Credit Card _____ $_____ Credit Card _____
$_____ Credit Card _____ $_____ Credit Card _____
$_____ Credit Card _____ $_____ Credit Card _____
$_____ Personal Loan _____ $_____ Personal Loan _____
$_____ Other_____ $_____ Other_____
$_____ Other_____ $_____ Other_____

$_____ Total Monthly Debt $_____ Total Monthly Debt

Combined Monthly Debt $_____

Take combined debt $_____ (factor each debt only once – if it is a joint debt list under the primary income earner only) and divide by the combined income $_____. The percentage _____% is the monthly debt-to-income ratio.

Figure 8:1 Sample Form – Credit Report Authorization and Release – HUD Public Release

CREDIT REPORT AUTHORIZATION AND RELEASE

Authorization is hereby granted to _____ to
obtain a standard factual data credit report through a credit-reporting agency chosen by
_____.

My signature below authorizes the release to the credit-reporting agency a copy of my
credit application, and authorizes the credit-reporting agency to obtain information
regarding my employment, savings accounts, and outstanding credit accounts (mortgages,
auto loans, personal loans, charge cards, credit unions, etc.)

Authorization is further granted to the reporting agency to use a Photostatted reproduction
of this authorization if necessary to obtain any information regarding the above-mentioned
information.

Applicants hereby request a copy of the credit report with any possible derogatory
information be sent to the address of present residence, and holds
_____ and any credit reporting
organization harmless in so mailing the copy requested.

Any reproduction of this credit authorization and release made by reliable means (for
example photocopy or facsimile is considered an original.

_____   _____
Borrower's Signature   Borrower's Signature
Date: Date:
SSN: SSN:

_____   _____
Borrower's Signature   Borrower's Signature
Date: Date:
SSN: SSN:

Figure 8:2 Sample Form – Credit Report Authorization and Release – HUD Public Release

Investors will review hundreds of potential investment packages. It is often considered a duty of the Note Broker to create an Analysis Worksheet on any potential note investment package being presented to the Investor.

This Analysis Worksheet will detail all of the specific items that will be of interest to the potential Investor. Organizing all of the details from the transaction documents will allow the Investor to quickly assess each package and compare the specifics of the package against the Investors target goals.

In the final analysis, Note Brokering is a service-based business and providing exceptional service to the Seller and the Investor is the essential component of your success. Any action that you take to simplify the process for the Investor is considered a service and will make the Investor more likely to find working with you a time-effective and desirable business opportunity. By creating a comprehensive analysis worksheet for each package you present, you allow the Investor to gain the transaction details in one convenient location and show respect for the time of your Investors.

Chapter

9

SUBMISSION ANALYSIS

SELLER OR REFERENCE NUMBER:_____

Broker:_____ Contact: _____

Address: _____ Phone: _____

NOTE DETAILS

Note Face Value: $_____ Initial Sales Price: $_____

Appraised Value: $_____ Monthly Payment: $_____

1st Payment Date: _____ Last Payment Date: _____

Balloon Scheduled $_____ Date of Balloon: _____

Payments Per Year: _____ Interest Rate: _____

BORROWER INFORMATION

Credit Score: _____ Credit Level: _____

Payment History on Note: _____ DTI Ratio: _____

Employer: _____ Employer: _____

No yrs. _____ Position: _____ No yrs. _____ Position: _____

Explanation of Credit Situation/Notes: _____

_____

_____

_____

DOCUMENTS

___Appraisal   ___Homeowners Insurance   ___Title Insurance

___Settlement Statement ___Amortization Schedule   ___Sales Contracts

___Note   ___Mortgage   ___Credit Consent

___Credit Report   ___Income Documentation   ___Payment History

___Analysis Worksheet   ___Other _____   ___Other _____

Figure 9:1 Sample Form – Submission Analysis

SUBMISSION ANALYSIS WORKSHEET KEY

Reference Number: Many transactions will require you to act as the negotiation liaison between the Investor and the Note Seller. To maintain the privacy between the parties it is best to provide only reference numbers early in the transaction.

You should assign each note package a reference number before submitting the package to the Investor.

Broker: You will enter the business name of the Note Brokerage for which you work. Even when you own the brokerage, you should enter the professional name under which you conduct business with the Investor.

Address: Enter the mailing address of your business.

Telephone: Your telephone contact information will be necessary to ensure a speedy communication process. Having your contact information readily available on the submission worksheet will save the Investor time when they must contact you in regards to your submission.

Additional ID: You may wish to include additional contact information depending on the structure of your business. This information should assist the Investor in speedy contact.

You might prefer email or FAX contact on all of your transactions particularly if you are a mobile Note Broker without a dedicated office location.

NOTE DETAILS

Note Face Value: The face value of the note will be the total principal figure due and payable as of the date of submission of the package.

This figure will act as the basis for the Investor's calculations.

Initial Sales Price: The original sales price incorporated into the note should be entered.

This figure allows the Investor to compare the current face value against the original sales price to determine the possible equity position of the borrower in the transaction.

Many Investors will also wish to confirm that the current face value is appropriate compared to the initial sales price, the down payment and the number of payments reported to have been made against the note.

Appraised Value: The appraised value will often be similar to the initial sales price.

The Investor will base a portion of their investment and discounting decisions on the appraised value as compared to the note face value.

Monthly Payment: The monthly payment is the monthly return the Investor will receive on their investment.

The Investor will compare the monthly payment figure entered times the number of payments remitted to verify the note face value is at the correct figure for the point in the transaction where the sale is being negotiated.

1ˢᵗ Payment Date: The Investor will wish to know the date the first payment was made under the note.

This date will be used for confirmation that the numbers provided are correct.

This date will also be used to calculate the seasoning on the note.

The seasoning is the length of time the note has been in existence and that payments have been made as agreed under the terms of the note.

Many Investors desire a note with a specific seasoning term.

Last Payment Date: The last payment date typically refers to the date the last payment was made on the note agreement. This allows the Investor to fine-tune the actual calculations on the transaction and to determine when the next payment is due.

Many Investors will complete note transactions quickly so the next payment due will frequently be paid to the Investors.

Balloon Scheduled Date of Balloon: Some Note Sellers will have negotiated a balloon term cash out on the seller held note.

This balloon is in place to allow the seller to obtain the total sum owed under the note at a particular point during the transactions.

Many privately funded sales are eligible for conventional financing after a certain period has elapsed.

The Investor will need to consider any balloon payments negotiated into the transaction.

The receipt of a lump sum balloon payment will effect the interest accumulations the Investor can expect to receive in the transaction as well as the term the Investor's capital will be involved in this particular investment.

Payments Per Year: The Investor will need to know the number of payments due under the note in a calendar year.

Some transactions will require the individual making payments remit the negotiated payments on a quarterly basis, others will require payments on a monthly basis.

The number of payments remitted per year allows the Investor to fine-tune calculations regarding their potential return and the term they can expect to wait before they receive payments against their capital.

Interest Rate: The interest rate assessed against the note will play a vital role in the total return on the capital investment in the note.

The potential return obtained through interest accumulations is included earlier in the course. You should review this material to gain a comprehensive understanding of why the interest rate must be accurately reported on the analysis worksheet.

BORROWER INFORMATION

Credit Score: Many lenders and Investors are using credit scores, as a final determination of the probability the borrower will make payments on the note as agreed. Details regarding the credit score and directions to locate the score are included earlier in the course.

Credit Level: Many Investors will use a practice termed blended grading to determine the approval level of a borrower. This blended system incorporates the credit score as well as specific details in the borrower's profile such as DTI Ratio's, actual payment history, LTV of the original note and other items. If your Investor partner uses a blended system, they will provide you with product approval guidelines to assist you in determining the level of the borrower.

Since the Credit Score incorporates many of these factors into the mathematical formulas that generate the borrower's score, many Investors will base their initial assessment on only the score.

Payment History: The payment performance of the individual making payments on the note will be an essential factor in predicting the future probability of payments being made as agreed.

Many Investors will require proof that the payments reported by the seller have been made as reported.

DTI Ratio: The Investor will calculate the DTI Ratio to assess the monthly cash flow of the individual making payments on the note.

> The lower the DTI Ratio the higher the individual's monthly cash flow.
>
> The higher the individual's monthly cash flow the better the probability that they will have the funds available to make payments on the note as agreed.

Employer: The employment history of both the borrower and any co-borrower listed on the note will be an important factor in the credit profile.

The stability of a borrower's employment history assists the Investor in predicting the future employment and therefore the maintenance of the current DTI Ratio and cash flow of the borrower.

Explanation of Situation:

A borrower with a less than stable employment history may have a higher probability of encountering financial difficulty during the term of the note.

This section is provided on many analysis worksheets to allow you to provide package details, which may effect the Investors purchase decisions.

Any compensating factors that exist in the package, any explanations for specific items and any additional information that may prove essential to the Investors decision should be included in this section.

The heading of this section is termed Explanation of Credit Situation/Notes but any item of importance to the Investor should be included here regardless of the specific type of information. You will be the best-informed individual involved in the transaction and it is up to you to provide the best possible package overview to the Investor.

DOCUMENTS

A checklist of included documents should be provided with any package submittal.

The completion of this checklist allows the Investor to scan the listing to determine what items of interest are included with the package.

If a particular item is not included, you should note the date that you expect to obtain that document on the line. This date provides the Investor with the ability to plan their workflow based on your expected submittal dates.

Chapter

10

HOW YOU PROFIT FROM NOTES

Each party involved in a Note Brokering process benefits from the transaction.

Sellers of the note benefit through the obtainment of a cash amount of money against the outstanding sum they are owed on the note agreement.

> Many sellers hold a note for reasons other than the simple desire to obtain a profitable return on the note in the form of interest.

> You will occasionally find a perceptive seller who holds long-term notes in an effort to capitalize on their funds. This is a rarity and most Sellers are eager to transfer the monthly payments and potential profit of a note to an Investor in exchange for the lump sum of cash they will receive.

Investors or Note Buyers will benefit by collecting a return on their investment that often exceeds any other potential investment opportunity available. To understand the benefits a Investor will receive you should carefully review the section detailing interest accumulations included earlier in the course. Essentially, the return of interest on the funds owed can double or even triple the Investors capital investment over the term of the note.

Kenney

Another method of immediate profit is the discounting of a note. We just explained the premise of the seller transferring the potential interest and penalty profit of a note in exchange for the cash lump sum received. Most sellers are also willing to discount the face value of a note in exchange for the cash sum received.

Example of a discount would be:

Seller held note value:	$45,000
Discount premium offered:	20%
Immediate note equity:	$ 9,000

There are two reasons the seller will be required to discount the face value of their note.

1.   The first reason is that the interests expected from the note are futures.

This means that the profit will be obtained at some point in the future and does carry some level of risk.

By discounting the face value of the note, the Investor generates an instant equity position in the property securing the note.

This protects the Investor's position in a manner similar to the loan to value process followed by conventional lenders.

By holding equity in the instrument that secures the note, the Investor is provided with a level of security against buyer default.

The common belief in the conventional mortgage industry is that the higher the portion of equity held in the property the lower the risk of borrower default.

The note the Investor will be purchasing has been negotiated and finalized. It is not possible for the Investor to return to the individual paying the note and negotiate a higher borrower equity position in the property. Therefore, the only method of Investor security left is to generate equity in the note through the discounting process.

Using the note scenario above you can see that if the property was valued at $45,000 and the note held by the seller was for the total $45,000 the property would be financed to 100% of its value. If the individual making payments on the note were to default or stop making payments the Seller would find it difficult to recoup their entire $45,000 at a foreclosure sale.

If the note is discounted 20%, the Investor holds a 20% equity position.

> What this means is that if the buyer makes all payments as agreed the Investor will achieve a 20% return on their investment without adding potential interest accumulations.

> More importantly, if the individual paying the note fails to pay as agreed and the Investor is forced to foreclose upon the property and offer it for sale to recoup their investment, the Investor has a 20% equity position in the property.

> This equity would allow the Seller to offer the property for sale at a discount off the value of the property. This increases the chances of the Investor making the sale and obtaining the return on their investment.

2.   The second consideration in the note discounting process is your position.

As a Note Broker, you will perform all of the activities needed to bring together the Seller and the Investor interested in purchasing the note.

The discounting process enables you to be paid for your work. Often an Investor will have a pre-set discount that they apply to the notes they purchase.

In the example above, the Investor may have agreed to pay 90% of the note face value.

$45,000   X   90%   = $40,500

The seller may have agreed to accept 80% of the face value of the note in a cash lump sum.

$45,000   X   80%   = $36,000

The difference between what the Investor is willing to pay and the seller is willing to accept will be your payment for the work you have performed to bring together the seller and the Investor.

$40,500   - $36,0000   = $ 4,500

It is up to you to determine the minimum cash out the seller will be willing to accept and to negotiate the discount in a manner that allows you to obtain your commission or payment.

You may request a flat fee payment in addition or in place of the commission built into the discount from the Investor, the Note Seller or both.

UNDERSTANDING COMMISSIONS

You now have an understanding the interest accumulation and equity position the Investor in a note will obtain.

You have a base knowledge of the benefits to the seller of obtaining a lump sum cash-out for the note held.

The next important factor you should focus on is the payment you will receive for your activity in the Note Brokering process.

You will perform a variety of activities in relationship to the Note Brokering process.

- You will advertise, research and market to locate potential Sellers interested in transferring their interest in a note.

- You will advertise, market and research to locate Investors interested in capitalizing on the notes available.

- You will gather all of the documentation needed by the Investor to insure that the note is a good investment and to secure the Investors interests in the note.

- You will negotiate the note discount premium with the seller of the note.

- You will negotiate the maximum premium the Investor is willing to pay against the face value of the note.

- You will perform many of the liaison functions necessary to complete the note transfer documents and inform the individual making payments on the note of the transfer.

Without your efforts in the transaction, chances are the transfer will never take place. You will typically:

- Locate a viable note.

- Negotiate the sale of the note with the Seller.

- Locate an interested Investor.

- Negotiate the discount cash-out with the Investor.

- Complete the steps required to make the transaction official.

You are one of the most important components to a successful transaction. As a vital component of the transaction, you should receive a premium payment for your services.

Numerous methods exist that enable you to negotiate your fees. You may use only one of the payment methods or you may negotiate a combination of payment options. If you are careful in your planning and negotiation, you may actually receive three different payments for each transaction you negotiate.

1. The first payment you might negotiate is a lump sum payment with the Investor for the service of locating a good note investment.

    This payment is also termed a finder's fee.

    A finder's fee is a pre-set agreement with the Investor that they will pay you a certain premium for locating a Seller interested in selling their position.
    Often the Investor will agree to pay you this premium regardless of the outcome of the transaction.

Some Investors do make the payment contingent on the completion of the deal while others will pay you a premium for bringing the Seller to their attention.

Those Investors who pay you the finder's premium often take over the transaction negotiations immediately and complete the transaction themselves.

> This allows you to collect your commission and move on to locating the next Seller.

> This is a quick pay method of Note Brokering and may be a fantastic opportunity early in your career.

You may also remain a part of the negotiation process. Seeing the process through to the end of the transaction and negotiating the sale offers another potential income for you. You should carefully consider the potential gains of staying a part of the transaction against the time investment required.

2. The second method of payment is to negotiate a commission with the seller for your activity in locating the Investor.

A seller is often willing to pay you a certain pre-set amount in exchange for your actions in locating potential Investors.

> This amount is usually contingent on the seller actually obtaining a cash out for the note from the Investor.

> This commission is typically paid at the time the note transfers.

When negotiating this type of commission you have one of two additional options.

> You may step away as soon as the Seller and the Investor are brought together. This allows the Investor and Seller to complete the negotiations of the details of the transaction themselves and allows you to begin searching for the next person holding a note and interested in receiving a cash-out sum for their note.
> You may also complete the payment agreement and remain a part of the negotiation process. By seeing the transaction through to completion you

actually, generate an additional income opportunity for yourself through the discount negotiation.

You must carefully weigh the time investment of assisting in the negotiation process against the potential gain to determine what method of brokering is best for you.

3.   The last form of commission you may receive is through the discount premium.

If the seller holds a note for $45,000 and is willing to accept a cash balance against the note of 80% of the face value, the seller will take $36,000 in exchange for their note.

You must assist the seller in locating an Investor who is willing to pay a minimum of 80% against the face value of the note.

If you locate an Investor willing to pay up to 90% against the face value of the note, you have an agreement on the part of the Investor to pay $40,500 for the $45,000 note held by the seller.

This leaves some cash on the table. The Investor is willing to bring $40,500 to the table. The seller is willing to walk away from the table

with $36,000. This leaves 10% of the face value of the note on the table.

Investor Transaction

$45,000   face value of the note
x   90% paid by the Investor
_____
$40,500   cash at closing -

Seller Transaction

$45,000   face value of the note
x   80% acceptable to the seller
_____
$36,000   seller cash at close

There remains $4,500 cash unaccounted for in the transaction.

The amount of money left on the table after the Investor has paid the amount agreed and the Seller receives the funds they negotiated as acceptable can be your money.
This is called building the commission and is the primary reason the Note Broker will assist in the finalized negotiations between the Investor and the Seller.

Chapter

11

THE SETTLEMENT

After you have negotiated the final terms with both the Seller and the Investor, you must arrange for a settlement or transfer. At times, all of the parties will sit at what is termed a round table settlement. Other times the Investor and the Seller will never meet. You must determine the best settlement strategy to employ with each transaction you negotiate.

When you arrange a settlement meeting where all of the individuals who are a party to the transactions will attend one meeting place, it is imperative that you have a solid working relationship with the Attorney or Settlement Company overseeing the meeting. At this type of settlement, all of the parties will be present. You have typically negotiated a commission, or even multiple commissions, into the transaction and you will not want either party to take specific note of the commission payments you have negotiated.

When you have negotiated a commission with both parties and/or built your commission into the discount figure you may be gaining payment for your services up to three times in the transaction.

The built-in commission or commission created in the difference between what you negotiate with the Investor as the cash-out of the note The amount you negotiate with the Seller as an acceptable lump sum for the note could actually be considered by both parties to be their money.

A pre-set finder's fee set with the Investor in exchange for locating viable note investments.

A pre-set finder's fee set with the Seller in exchange for your efforts in assisting them in selling the note.

The best possible settlement meeting where all parties attend will occur following a process such as:

1. The Settlement Company generates a settlement statement detailing the transaction specifics of all parties.

2. The Settlement Company provides you with a settlement statement so that you can review and approve all of the transaction figures, including your commission.

3. The Settlement Company notifies the Investor of the exact dollar amount due at the settlement and confirms the time and date of the meeting.

4. The Settlement Company notifies the Seller of the exact dollar figure they can expect to receive at the settlement and confirms the date and time of the meeting.

5. The Investor provides the Settlement Company with a certified check or wire transfer for the money due.

    It is usually desirable to have the transaction money in the hands of the settlement company prior to the date of the settlement.

    This allows the settlement company to divide the funds as outlined in the settlement statement and issue checks for any outstanding balances, commission figures and in the amount due to the Seller.

6. All individuals who have a part in the transaction, including you, will arrive at the settlement meeting at the time and date set for the settlement.

7.   All Sellers who will sign the documents and the Investor must provide the settlement agent with proof of identity before the signing of any document.

8.   The settlement official will typically provide the Seller with a copy of the security instrument and a transfer agreement that transfers the Seller's interest in the note.

> The Seller signs the documents transferring any rights and interest agreed upon with their signature.

> All parties named on the note and security agreement must sign these documents.

9.   The settlement agent will then tell the former Sellers that this is the end of their portion of the transfer.

> At times, the settlement agent will provide the former Seller with their check at the settlement meeting.

> Since all figures were disclosed to the Seller before the meeting, there is no need to discuss the actual amount of the check.

> At other times, the settlement agent will inform the former Seller that their checks will be available after all transfer documents have been confirmed and recorded.

> When this occurs, the settlement agent will arrange for the former Seller to return for their check at a specific time.

10.   The Seller is now finished with their part of the transaction and may leave the settlement meeting.

11.   The settlement agent will then obtain transfer acceptance signatures from the Investor.

> The need for these signatures will vary depending on the type of transaction.

> The Investor may have other documentation they will need to complete depending on the type of transaction being finalized.

Upon completion of all of the signatures, the settlement agent will explain the period for the recording of the new assignment agreement.

12. Since the Investor has provided the funds for the transaction before the meeting, the Investor may then leave the meeting.

13. At this time, the settlement agent will issue any additional checks and payments as outlined on the settlement statement generated previously and approved by you.

   One such check will be your commission check.

- You will note that there was never a time at the meeting that the settlement agent divulged any transaction specifics to either party.

   All of the specifics, dollar figures and transaction requirements were provided to each party before the meeting, thereby limiting the potential for misunderstanding at the settlement meeting.

Not all meetings will flow this smoothly. It is imperative that you strive for smooth settlements. By building a strong relationship with your settlement partners, you will ensure that each settlement proceeds in a smooth and efficient manner with all parties walking away from the meeting with the opinion that both you and the settlement agent are competent professionals who provided exceptional service.

Following the settlement meeting there are some follow-up activities that must be completed. The settlement agent will handle some of these activities, others will fall to the new Seller. You may wish to offer follow-up services to your Investor. Any service you perform above those provided by your competition will improve your customer satisfaction (Investor) and promote future business with that Investor as well as future referral business.

Some of the activities that must be completed following the settlement meeting:

- The settlement agent will record any documents that must be recorded at the appropriate courthouse of record.

- The settlement agent will issue all checks required for the completion of the transaction.

These may include payment to service providers such as appraisers and credit report agencies that were used in the transaction and will typically include costs for the recording of the required documents at the courthouse.

Your commission check will also be included as part of the checks written after closing.

- The new Investor will contact the insurance company who holds the insurance policy securing the collateral of the note.

  The Investor will want to ensure they are added as a loss payee on the insurance policy.

  Adding the Investor as a loss payee ensures that the Investor will receive the first insurance settlement payment in the event the collateral property is damaged or destroyed by a covered cause such as a fire.

- The new Investor will issue a notification letter to the individual making payments on the note.

  This is similar to a mortgage servicing transfer disclosure in the conventional home finance process.

  This notification letter will inform the individual making payments on the note that the note has transferred.

  The notification should notify the individual that no alterations have been made to the terms of the note.

  The notification will provide information regarding the new location for the remittance of note payments.

- If the note that has been transferred to the Investor is not a first lien on the property securing the note, the Seller will want to contact the senior lien holder.

  This contact should request that the senior lien holder notify the new Seller of any issues that arise in the future regarding payment on the senior note or other issues that exist with regard to borrower performance.

This notification of performance issues on the part of the individual making payments on the note allows the new Seller to protect their interests in the event the borrower is in danger of defaulting on their primary lien or in the event of other hazards exist that may put the Seller's investment at risk.

- The Investor then begins accepting the payments due under the note and moves onto their next investment opportunity.

- You are then able to begin the process of locating and negotiating the sale of your next note.

Chapter

12

STARTING YOUR BUSINESS

Congratulations. You have reached the point in the coursework that marks the obtainment of the knowledge and skills that will enable you to enter the profession of Note Brokering. You have completed the chapters that provided the essential elements upon which you will build the framework of your career. Now you must make the decisions that will map the strategy you will follow to achieve top-producing status within the Note Brokering Field. There are both personal business decisions and professional activities you must perform before you begin marketing for your first note.

What is my specialty?

We have provided you with many ideas regarding the most common types of notes available for your brokerage business. You must create a business plan that provides you with the opportunity to work with the notes you feel best able to negotiate.

- Many beginning Note Brokers find it easiest to begin with a note specialty with which they have a basic familiarity

- Others prefer to begin their business with the most readily available forms of notes.

Regardless of you specialty you should begin your business with a focused plan. Attempting to generalize and broker all types of notes from day one may provide you with a surplus of initial deals to place, but will not provide you with the opportunity to focus 100% of your efforts in a particular type of note.

- Focused effort on one or two types of notes early in your career will allow you to create a reputation for thorough knowledge and exceptional capability within that note specialty.

- Once you have become an expert on one or two types of notes, then you should consider the expansion of your specialty.

Focusing on a particular venue during the first days in your new career provides another benefit.

You will build strong relationships with the Investors who specialize in the purchase of that type of note.

Your business will only be as strong as the relationships you build with your investment partners.

When you begin the process of seeking out potential Investors you will see that there are literally hundreds of Investors available for each type of note you have available for sale.

By limiting your venue choice, you have the ability to close solid deals with your Investor partners and to build a strong relationship with them.

Your reputation with the Investor will increase when you provide many, solidly qualified packages, to that Investor.

Diffusing your attention over many types of notes and with many types of Investors early in your career, may limit your ability to provide the solid, focused attention each package.

Who will buy my packages?

After you have determined your note specialty, you will wish to locate the best possible Investors for your note type. Each Investor will have a series of submission guidelines and processes they prefer. A general Internet search will provide you with the contact information for hundreds of potential Investor partners. Contact each partner whose basic information matches your chosen specialty. These Investors will typically have an information package they are able to send you that details their:

Preferred note parameters

Discount processes

Commission terms

Submission process outline

Closing preferences

Note specialties

And other information deemed important to the type of note being offered

You should review each Investor package carefully to determine the ones that are offering the best possible programs to meet your business needs. You may find that you must experiment with the various Investors until you locate the ones that will match your business style and note preferences the best.

Before beginning the marketing of notes, you must notify the County and State of your new business. Most States now have an online application for registering a new business. The application will also provide you with information regarding other licensure and registration requirements within your chosen State of operation. If you are unable to locate the required information through the internet web site, you may also contact your local Chamber of Commerce, County Courthouse or Small Business Association for the necessary applications and processes to open a business in your area.

Where will I work?

Earlier we mentioned that you might set up your business in as large or as small of a manner as you prefer and as your financial situation allows.

- You must remember that, as a professional Note Broker people will perceive you as having money

- You are in the business of selling money and have entered a professional career

- You must always ensure that your image promotes the best possible vision of you and your new company

  This image presentation does not mean that you must spend a lot of money.

  This does mean that you must strive to present the most professional appearance possible at all times.

You should obtain a dedicated telephone line that is located in a quiet area and attached to a voice mail or message system that only promotes your business. The advanced marketing skill course provides detailed training regarding Business Etiquette, Professionalism and Appropriate Telephone Skills. If you are unsure of your skills in this area, you should commit to completing an Advanced Business and Marketing Skills course as soon as possible to ensure you are presenting all potential business partners with the most professional image you can present.

Marketing Strategy

In the following pages, we will lead you in developing your first marketing plan.

The primary task, before you begin marketing for your first note, is developing a system for tracking the effect of your marketing efforts.

Early in your career, you will spend the balance of your time marketing.

You will complete a variety of tasks such as making contacts, building relationships, and getting your name out to your target groups.

The abundance of time available early in your career enables you to take the opportunity to experiment.

You will be able to use a variety of marketing methods to determine what works best for you.

Each person's strengths and weaknesses are different and therefore each person's marketing plan should be different.

Sometime in the first 90 days as a Note Broker, you will need to begin redirecting the bulk of your efforts to processing and closing note transfers. At that time, it will become very important to expend your marketing efforts in the areas that bring you the strongest return.

To determine where your valuable time and energies should be expended you will need solid market penetration figures. As time management becomes vital to your continued success, these figures will allow you to determine, based on solid tracking numbers, exactly what marketing efforts provide success for you!

During the training, we recommended that you use a pre-qualification data sheet for each potential note-transfer transaction. The top of this sheet contains a place to note the referral source of the inquiry. If you have completed this data entry field, you will have an excellent overview of what marketing efforts have yielded a return.

You may wish to develop a different system that works for you. An excellent computerized system is the ACT! Program. This program offers an enlarged database that you customize to include all pertinent information about a note transaction. These programs will also generate reports upon request. These reports can give you your market referral numbers at the touch of a button.

Experiment with different systems to find the tracking method that will work best for your work style. Just be sure you HAVE a system. Whatever method of tracking you use, knowing what brings in the clients and what is a non-returning waste of your time, money and efforts is well worth the time involved in creating and utilizing the tracking plan.

Choosing Marketing Areas

There are seven beginning marketing options with proven results for a Note Broker.

Advertising

Group Presentations

Flier/Mail Campaigns

Courthouse Research

Wine and Dine

Telemarketing

Networking

Your market plan may contain only a couple of these options or a combination of all of these options.

You will need to balance your strengths, budget, market conditions and time to determine how you wish to work within your particular market.

Advertising

Your first goal is exposure. Unless your target market knows who you are, where you are and what you can do for them, they will never call!

Print Media and Radio Media are the two most common forms of advertising for a beginning Note Broker.

Radio Advertisements are designed to promote name recognition.

Print advertisements are designed to convey information.

As a beginning Note Broker, you will probably want to focus on print. This allows you to leave the more costly radio advertising and name recognition creation for a later point in your new business expansion.

The other advertising methods are typically more costly and you will want to scrutinize your profit sheets to determine exactly what advertising media will be best for you.

> Radio and television advertisements will build name recognition in the market place.

> Print advertisements will typically bring personal recognition and provide the vital ability to convey specific information to your target groups.

Many newspapers offer a free "new in business" advertisement. This brief blurb tells the public that you are now in business. The advertisement should tell the public: who you are, your specialty and your contact information. This is an excellent first step in getting your name out there. Best of all it is usually offered free.

If you are joining an existing Note Broker, you can also place a Welcome Aboard advertisement. These advertisements can sometimes be obtained from the media source at a reduced cost in the hopes of generating future advertising business. Even if you are opening your own Note Brokerage, a welcome aboard advertisement can still assist you in placing that first all-important notice to the public that you are now in the business of assisting them in obtaining their note cash-out needs.

A welcome aboard advertisement should look something like this:

<u>Company Name</u>
is proud to Welcome <u>Your Name</u>
a certified Note Broker.

Specializing in <u>Type of Note</u>
sales, <u>Your Name</u> is available for
a FREE analysis of your note!

Give <u>Your First Name</u> a call today and welcome him/her aboard! <u>Telephone Number</u>

You will note the advertisement gives:

- Your company (where you are)

- Your name (who you are)
- Your title (showing your capabilities)

- Your specialty (notifying your target market that you are here FOR them)

- A FREE offer (nothing will make your phone ring faster than the word FREE!)

- And an order to call today (people sometimes need permission to call and instructions on how and when to contact you to feel comfortable taking that first step.)

If you are able to place an advertisement specific to you, you will want to make every dollar count.

- Research ALL the print media in your area.

    Example: Primary newspapers, Real Estate Guides, Bargain Shopper Style Newspapers and anything else specific to your region

- Determine the target market and circulation of the media you are considering. You will then want to assess how that circulation compares with your target market needs.

- Assess the cost of advertising.

- Review the advertisements that are bringing success to other Note Brokers to determine what they are doing that works well and where you could incorporate improved tactics to increase the success margin.

After you know what you can spend, make the final decision as to where you wish to place your advertising.

- Carefully weigh the cost of the advertisement against the circulation and market of each media source.

    You should quickly determine that one or two options outstrip the competition.

- Now it is time to write your first advertisement.

    You will want your advertisement to be understandable, efficient and direct. Bear in mind, when composing the advertisement, the majority of the population comprehends at no more than an 8th grade reading level.

A sample advertisement might be:

Are you tired of accepting monthly payments?
Did you know that a note is a valuable cash generator?
Did you know that there are people ready to give you cash for your note today?
Can you think of something you could do tomorrow with cash in your hands?

I can help!
Call <u>your name</u> at <u>your company and telephone number</u>
for your FREE analysis of your note and let me help put cash in your hands today!

- Notice the attention-getting header that targets a market currently receiving payments.

- The questions included are those that are actually the most common excuses for why people have not already sold their note.

- Followed by a question that makes the Seller consider what they would do with their cash settlement.

- A simple and strong statement I CAN HELP.

- Lastly, you are giving them permission to call and you are stressing the word FREE.

  Many people cannot resist free especially when it is tied to something they truly want – the cash for their note in their hands-immediately.

- The advertisement is short (therefore less costly), concise and simple to understand.

An advertisement, which contains all of the characteristics of the one above, should make your telephone begin to ring very quickly.

The last item you should consider before placing any advertisement is that there are laws regarding appropriate advertising. These laws limit the discrimination against individuals through advertising.

The Federal Fair Housing Act prohibits the use of discriminatory advertising or advertisements that state a preference for a particular type of person. You may not advertise in a manner meant to attract or deter a potential client based on race, color, religion, sex, handicap, familial status or national origin.

HUD released a clarification of acceptable words and phrases, which can be used in real estate related advertisements. You must use caution when composing your advertising so as not to include any item that is discriminatory in nature. More information regarding acceptable advertising is included in the Advanced Note Brokerage Marketing Course or directly from HUD.

The nature of advertising allows you a broad spectrum in which to operate. It is important to remember that discrimination in real estate practice is illegal. Many of your transactions will relate to the real estate industry since Mortgage Notes are the most common Note Brokering opportunity you will see. Providing you are not targeting particular strata of society for either positive or negative effect, staying within the guidelines is relatively easy.

Federal Agencies evaluate their policies and programs on a regular basis to determine any modifications and executive orders that must be added as a protected class under the fair housing laws. You should review these policies and laws frequently to ensure your advertisements remain within the guidelines.

The last important component of advertising is that you must provide repetition to obtain results. Most people do not call the first or even the second time they see or hear an advertisement. To be effective, an advertising campaign must be repeated at least 10-12 times to generate an action on the part of the reader. In your case, you are looking for an analysis contact.

Your chosen advertising venue will have trained account representatives who can assist you with determining market penetration figures, the target market for their venue and even assist you in composing the proper advertisement. You should use the knowledge and experience gained by these professional service providers. You are a professional Note Broker and understand your business better than any other individual with whom you come in contact. You should compose the content of the advertisement. These service providers are professionals within the advertising industry and understand their business better than you will be able to, since your focus must be elsewhere. You should rely on their experience and professional knowledge to assist you in making every advertising dollar count.

Group Presentations

Group presentations are an excellent method of conveying your information to a large group of people at the same time. Before you begin planning your carefully composed and rehearsed presentation, you will need to think about the following "tips":

- Think of a presentation as a performance.

  You might want to entertain, motivate and inspire your audience all at the same time.

  Instead, you should carefully consider which your primary objective is and never lose focus.

- Grab your audience.

  Do not give the audience the opportunity to lose interest.

  Grab them from the beginning with a "hook".

    A hook is a statement that conveys why they, not you, need know this information.

    Everyone wants to know "what's in it for me."

- Engage your audience.

  Most presentations are boring.

  Keep the presentation moving along and engaging and your audience will be more responsive.

- Make eye contact with your audience – even before you begin to speak.

- Keep your presentation moving

  State your background.

  Hit them with the facts on what you do and what you can do for them.

Finish.

Most presentations fail because the speaker tries to include too much information.

- Use a strong speaking voice.

  Even if you feel uncomfortable, a strong tone will inspire confidence.

  A mousy tone will cause your audience to lose interest.

- DO NOT wiggle, rock or pace.

  Transfer excess energy to your voice, expression and hands.

- Control your desire to rush.

  Slow down.

  Use pauses.

  Let the audience into your presentation.

- Do not walk in unprepared

  An interested audience will turn your presentation into a discussion.

  Know the answers to any question they may ask.

  If you do not know the answer, do not "fake it". It is always better to say, "I don't know the answer to that question at the present time... let me get back to you." Make sure you find the answer and get back to them – SOON!

- Change the tempo.

  Changes in tempo help an audience maintain interest.

  Emphasize what is important by saying it more slowly and more loudly.

  For points of lesser importance, speak more softly and more quickly.

- Do not forget to "close" your presentation.

  Review your important points and finish with a memorable closing line.

- Follow your close with a thanks and farewell.

  Leave behind a good feeling about you and your presentation.

  Resist the urge to stay and chat.

When creating your presentation it is important to establish the goals of your audience. You would not give the same presentation to a Landlord who is just considering holding a note as you would at a seminar of Real Estate Agents who assist buyers and sellers in negotiating home sales. The key to each presentation is what you can do FOR THEM.

Our advanced Note Brokerage Marketing program contains a full array of presentations customized to the most common groups you will market throughout your career. You may create your own presentations by simply focusing on the idea of what is most important to your audience.

For a current Seller, the answer is the obtainment of an immediate lump sum of cash. For a Real Estate Agent the answer is the ability to close more homes by negotiating a seller held note, which can then be sold to a Investor.

Flier/Mail Campaigns

Direct print campaigns can be aimed toward affinity groups or your prospective clients. Either way, the goal of a direct print campaign is to have your name and information in front of the people that you are targeting.

Examples of affinity groups you may target include:

Landlord Associations

Financial Planners

Personal Injury Attorneys

FSBO'S

Real Estate Agencies

Prime Lenders

Anyone and everyone who has contact with the same group of clients you do are perfect for a direct media campaign.

When developing a flier/mail campaign you will want to construct direct, concise messages that will hold the attention of the target.

You will also want to vary your approach. Sending a letter every week for 10 weeks is not the correct way to approach a contact. Perhaps send a letter, followed by a postcard and then follow up with a personal visit to deliver a flier. Changing your method of approach reduces the possibility of boring your target.

Before beginning a direct marketing campaign, make certain the contacts you plan to use are fresh and exciting. New Note Brokers sometimes purchase ready-made marketing flier programs. Many of these programs include only the same, stale fliers and letters used by hundreds of Note Brokers in previous years. Your market will not find these re-used marketing tools interesting. This is not to say that it is wrong to purchase a pre-created program. Most of the programs offered are created by marketing professionals who have a comprehensive understanding of your business. This is to day that you should make certain any marketing tool you use is the newest and is fresh within your market.

Each contact should convey a different message of interest to the target. Always stress what you can do to increase their business or reputation. Once you have established personal contact, give them an opportunity to refer to you. Perhaps drop off a fill in form that allows them to list any person they feel could benefit from your service. Be sure the target is very clear regarding what you CAN do before asking to be allowed to get near their clients.

We recommend that you target one or two groups to start.

Develop your entire contact campaign before initiating the first contact. A recommended number of initial contacts are a minimum of one contact per week for six consecutive weeks.

Your ultimate goal with these contacts is to build to the point where you are comfortable requesting and they are comfortable referring joint clients.

Developing the Campaign

- Determine why your focus group would benefit by sending clients to you.

Example: We will detail a Personal Injury Attorney as an example.

Personal Injury Settlements are often complex and the injured party will frequently accept a periodic payment against the settlement award won.

Personal Injury tends to create financial strain causing blemishes on the credit report.

At the time of the settlement agreement, periodic payments may have seemed like the most sensible solution to the injured party. Over time, financial needs may arise that require a larger lump sum of cash than that provided through the periodic payments.

You can negotiate the sale of all or only a portion of the payments received.

Many settlements arrange for payments over a period up to 20 years.

The injured party may desire a total cash out of their agreed upon payments. This would entail negotiating the sale of all 20 years worth of payments.

At other times, the injured party may need only a portion of their settlement in a lump sum. This entails negotiating the sale of only a portion of the settlement such as 5 years worth of expected payments. This portioned sale may not be an option that the personal injury attorney knows about and is a very good highlight point to include in your campaign.

By providing the Personal Injury Attorney the opportunity to provide cash-out referrals to their clients, you assist the Attorney in providing customer service. This is an added benefit to the Attorney in that they can improve their customer service and future referral business at no cost by promoting your Note Brokering capability.

- Develop a program to convey those reasons to the target partner.

Develop your mail/flyer campaign based on the reasons you generated earlier.

Step 1:   Begin with a letter of introduction, telling who you are, your specialty and a few basic program guidelines targeted toward settlement cash-out.

Close with an explanation of how this benefits his clients and reduces the strain periodic payments can sometimes place on his clients.

Step 2:   The next contact might include a flyer emphasizing the points covered in your letter. Stop by his office to drop it off personally.

Step 3:   If you get the opportunity to speak directly to the Attorney when delivering your flier, send a follow up thank you card. If not, send a postcard reminding the Attorney of the important points of your letter and flier.

Step 4:   Your next contact should be a letter requesting a meeting to discuss which of the Attorney's clients you will be able to help.

You will want to have a carefully prepared presentation available in case the Attorney is interested in meeting with you immediately.

Step 5:   Whether you arrange a face-to-face interview with the Attorney or not, re-cap the presentation in a simple booklet form and hand deliver it to the office.

Step 6:   Next, you will want to ask for referrals.

Make this easy for the Attorney.

Create a form for easy entry of client's names and telephone numbers. Do not ask for every piece of information you will need to work with these clients. The basic contact information is all you should request to keep the process simple for your referring partner.

Another option is to drop off some "referral coupons" offering a discount on fees or simply a free analysis of their situation to any client bearing that coupon. It may be easier for the Attorney to hand out your coupons to his clients and let them contact you than it is for the Attorney to take the time to give you the information needed to contact his clients.

If, at this point, you have received referrals from your target be certain to keep them informed of the progress of the package. Even when you feel the information you have to convey is not vital to the referral source, they may feel differently.

Remember, each time you initiate a contact to convey progress, you are putting yourself in the forefront of the referral sources mind. In the forefront of their mind is exactly where you need to be if you expect continued referrals!

Again, if you are not comfortable developing your own series of print contacts there are many great systems available for purchase that incorporate some of the ideas above. Our system is patterned closely to the process we described and includes all of the mentioned affinity groups and more. Always be sure the system you are purchasing is newly generated or recently updated so that you are not simply using old, out-dated fliers and letters that the referral partner has seen many times in the past.

Wine and Dine

Everyone loves to be treated to a lunch or special event. As a Note Broker, people perceive you as having money. Let's face it – you sell money and therefore are inextricably linked to money in people's minds.

This is a more costly marketing technique that you will have to consider carefully to determine if the benefits outweigh the costs.

The primary benefit to taking a referral source to breakfast or lunch is that you will have a captive audience throughout the meal. This is a perfect opportunity to emphasize how you can improve their business. Be sure to do this in a non-aggressive manner. In some regions of the country, discussing business over a meal is considered inappropriate. You will want to assess the trends in your area and act accordingly.

An additional benefit is that once a person has eaten a meal with another they feel more connected. The more connected this affinity partner feels with you the more likely they are to remember you the next time they have a client who can use your help.

Telephone Marketing

Many states have now implemented a do not call list. You will want to confirm whether your state has such a list and if so gain access to guarantee that you are not marketing to people who have requested they be removed for all such lists.

If telephone marketing is available in your area, it is a great method of capitalizing on unused evening hours to create a larger client base.

Lists are readily available through marketing services that spend their efforts compiling target lists of prospects within your group. You can customize the list you request and buy as many or as few contacts as you wish. These lists, while better constructed than other options, are often rather costly. You will have to weigh the benefits verses the costs for yourself.

Another method of obtaining contact sheets for your area is the County Courthouse. Most courthouses provide, for a nominal fee, seller held mortgages listed on their records. You can customize this list by region, by year of closing, sometimes even by value of the mortgage.

Be sure to target mortgages written far enough in the past for some equity build-up to have occurred. Your Investor partner may also have seasoning requirements for any mortgage that they plan to purchase. You will want to be certain you contact those sellers who hold a mortgage created within the appropriate time.

Complete telephone-marketing programs and scripts are available. We have scripts customized toward note marketing as part of our advanced marketing programs. If you choose to purchase a telephone-marketing package, you should always be certain that the program offers scripts for both incoming and outgoing calls. One of the primary factors that you must remember is that much of your business will be conducted over the telephone. Most of us are comfortable on the telephone but have not taken the time to learn skills such as conversational control training and information extraction knowledge. These skills will be vital to your career success. A worthwhile marketing program will incorporate training that includes these and other telephone skills.

Networking

Perhaps the easiest of all marketing methods is simple networking.

Every person you meet has a home. Whether they hold a note today or not, they may have the opportunity to create a seller held note in the future. The knowledge that there is a potential source for ready cash if they create such a note may actually cause the seller to enter into a note transaction. This creates a future market for your business that will directly influence your success and growth in the years to come. The individuals who are note homeowners still require housing. These individuals may be renting for a variety of reasons but one of the most common is the inability to obtain conventional mortgage financing. By educating these people regarding seller held mortgage notes and the ability the seller may gain to transfer their interest in the notes at some point in the future you may create another ready-made Note Brokering scenario for your future.

Every person you meet has an additional network of family and friends – nearly everyone you meet will know someone who either collects payments or makes payments on a note of some type. The ability to generate conversations among peer groups regarding your business offerings is an essential key to growth and note sourcing.

Whether at your church, grocery store, mechanics or doctors office, you will meet people who may need your help. Make an extra effort to initiate conversations wherever you go.

Remember   tell people what you do – they cannot know you can be of service to them unless you tell them.

Always   carry business cards.

Always   have a pre-qualification questionnaire nearby! You will be amazed at how many people are willing to be pre-qualified and where!

Generate a Marketing Plan

Now that you have the information concerning initial marketing options, you may begin creating your marketing plan. At the end of this section is a sample-marketing month for a new Note Broker. You will need to purchase or create a schedule page that divides each day into hourly segments.

- First review the marketing options detailed in the preceding text.

- Determine which options you would like to put into effect first.

- Weigh each method and allocate it with a certain amount of time in your overall scheduling budget.

  Remember to allow time in your schedule for continued study of state and judicial requirements and the guidelines provided by each Investor with whom you plan to work.

- Begin filling in your schedule.

- Budget the appropriate amount of time for each task you wish to accomplish.

- Treat each task on your schedule as an appointment.

  Treat each marketing task as a place you must be and an activity you must perform regardless of weather conditions, other time pressures or your nervousness on a given day.

- Now begin your career as a Note Broker!

Kenney

<u>Sales Call Summary</u>

Date: _____Prospect Name: _____

Time: _____Purpose: _____

Outcome: _____

_____

Action Plan: _____

Date: _____Prospect Name: _____

Time: _____Purpose: _____

Outcome: _____

_____

Action Plan: _____

Date: _____Prospect Name: _____

Time: _____Purpose: _____

Outcome: _____

_____

Action Plan: _____

Sample Training Plan/Marketing Strategy
Month 1

Overview training program	Materials Review – Assess current knowledge	Basic Study	Basic Study	Complete Exercises Pre-qualifying a package
Phone Skills – Practice Pre-qualification Questionnaire	Study Marketing Techniques	Create Marketing Plan	Send Introduction to Newspaper	Create advertising campaign
Create Fliers, ads, mailers and other needed marketing tools.	Create Fliers, ads, mailers and other needed marketing tools.	Create Fliers, ads, mailers and other needed marketing tools.	Solidify marketing plan Develop operations system/ organize	Review all materials assessing for comprehension
Review specific product matrixes as provided by Investors	Review specific product matrixes as provided by Investors	Call on first face-to-face affinity group	Send Mailer to first by-mail affinity group	Place Advertising Plan month 2 marketing program

Managing your Pipeline

A pipeline is the number of active note files you have open at any given time. The purpose of tracking a pipeline is to move note packages through the steps required to achieve a closed transaction.

Many Note Brokers allow important leads and pre-qualifications to fall through the cracks, failing to follow up on possible sources of business.

Other Note Brokers forget important tasks that must be completed on a package and are in a rush to accomplish them at the last possible moments.

By keeping a weekly pipeline report, you will know at the beginning and end of each week exactly where each package on your desk is in the process. You will want to create a tracking form or system customized for your use. Some individuals prefer a paper pipeline that they can keep in a prominent place and fill in as needs arise. Other individuals prefer a computerized program such as the ACT! program, which will keep all tasks and status readily available. As you become more experienced, you will discover methods that work best for you.

Because of properly managing your pipeline, you will know exactly what follow up or reminders are required on your note packages. We have an intricate system of reminders available with our advanced marketing program but you are very capable of creating your own program.

The most important benefit of managing your pipeline properly is the ability to estimate your income.

You will be aware at all times of what note packages are preparing to close and what packages you can expect to close in the following month.

Tracking and Contact Management

Tracking each action on every note package is a vital activity. As mentioned earlier you may purchase a software system that will aid in this process, your program may include a section to enter information and status notes or you may choose to track all actions manually.

You will find the completion of pipeline reports, estimation of income and remembering the details of a specific note package and what actions you took and when is much easier if you keep sufficient records.

It is important that you realize that today you may remember the details of each note in your pipeline but as your pipeline grows in the coming months, you will find this more difficult.

A Note Broker who is properly organized will be more successful for many reasons. The most obvious is that they will not allow packages to fall through the cracks for lack of attention.

Following is a simplistic file tracking form that can be attached to the front of each note file for quick reference.

FILE TRACKING LOG

DATE	ACTION	BY

ANSWERS TO COMMON QUESTIONS

The Note Seller will have many questions for you throughout the negotiation process. You should have a series of answers available that provide the answers to the Note Seller's questions while allowing you to maintain control of the conversation. A complete training program on conversational control is included in the Advanced Marketing Course program and if this is an area, you feel you must fine-tune, you should commit to completing a program of this type to assist you with your advanced business practices and to promote professionalism and success. In this, basic course, we will provide you with some strategic answers to the most common questions your Note Seller may ask during a negotiation interview.

Regardless of the question asked by the Seller, your best tactic is to answer the question with a pre-qualification question of your own. The pre-qualification analysis worksheet will assist you in staying on track during the conversation. You should always remember that most individuals holding a note do not fully comprehend the Note Brokering business. It is up to you to lead the conversation exactly where you, as the professional, know it must go in order to assist the Seller in obtaining those goals. The conversation must always lead to the obtainment of the information you will need to analyze and pre-qualify the package.

Q.   What do you pay for notes?

The question of what you actually offer the Seller in exchange for the note will be contingent on many factors.

These include

- the status of the note
- value of the note
- the credibility and stability of the individual making payments on the note
- the security held against the note
- even your commission

You should never provide a cash value or percentage figure during the first conversation with a Seller.

The Seller does not understand the detailed factors that are assessed to determine the actual offer on a note. You will probably not be able or even wish to educate the

Seller regarding every facet of the qualification process. However, you must assure the Seller that your payment negotiations are fair and provide a limited amount of information regarding the note analysis process. A simple method of handling this question would be:

A. That is a very good question. Many factors affect the actual cash value of your note. We consider the note itself, the borrower, the appraisal, even your personal situation. You might even decide that you only wish to sell a portion of your note and keep the rest.

Do you have a few minutes to answer some questions so we can determine just how much cash you can get?

Q. What does it mean when you say you buy notes?

This type of question is the perfect lead in to your business pre-qualification sheet. You will immediately ask if the person calling holds a note.

A. Do you have a note agreement where you are accepting payments against money owed to you?

Q. Do I have to pay points and closing costs?

Again most individuals do note fully comprehend the Note Brokering business. Many of the Sellers will have experienced the home mortgage lending process so they will comprehend fees and points. You should answer within the frame of reference of the caller.

A. There are never any points on a note transfer with our Investors and we take care of all of the closing costs. If your note meets the guidelines the buyer is looking for, you simply attend the settlement and collect your lump-sum check. Do you have a few minutes so we can determine if your note meets our needs?

Q. What is the discount rate?

This is a great question.

The Seller asking this question already has some basic knowledge of the type of transaction you can negotiate. It is better to address the question of Investor returns with an individual who does understand the note process.

If the individual asks this question, you should not automatically commit to a figure. You should assure the caller that your discount rate is competitive with that of other, similar Investors. You should then explain the need for specific information before providing a discount estimate.

A.   Our discount rate is very competitive and often it is much lower than that of other Investors, however, it does vary depending on the type of note you hold and the actual status of the note. Do you have a few minutes to answer some questions so I can calculate your discount rate?

Q.   How long does all this take?

This question tells you that you have an individual who is motivated to complete the transaction.

You must place the time expectations back on the shoulders of the caller since the first step in the process requires a commitment on their part to provide the necessary information and documents for a complete note analysis.

A.   The process is typically very short, but the actual number of days will depend on you. I will need some basic information to give to the Investor. Can we meet at _____ to review the *(insert documentation request customized around the type of note)*? I should be able to give you a good time estimate after I have reviewed the note.

GLOSSARY OF TERMS

1-year ARM: An adjustable-rate mortgage (ARM) that has an initial interest rate for one year, and thereafter has an adjustment interval of one year. The adjustment is based on comparison interest caps and the indexed rate

3/1 ARM: An adjustable-rate mortgage (ARM) that has an initial interest rate for three years, and thereafter has an adjustment interval of one year. The adjustment is based on comparison interest caps and the indexed rate.

5/1 ARM: An adjustable-rate mortgage (ARM) that has an initial interest rate for five years, and thereafter has an adjustment interval of one year. The adjustment is based on comparison interest caps and the indexed rate

7/1 ARM: An adjustable-rate mortgage (ARM) that has an initial interest rate for seven years, and thereafter has an adjustment interval of one year. The adjustment is based on comparison interest caps and the indexed rate

10/1 ARM: An adjustable-rate mortgage (ARM) that has an initial interest rate for ten years, and thereafter has an adjustment interval of one year. The adjustment is based on comparison interest caps and the indexed rate

Abstract of Title: A written history of all the transactions that bear on the title to a specific piece of land An abstract of title covers the time from when the property was first sold to the present. Used by the Title Company to produce a title binder

Acceleration Clause: The section of a mortgage document that allows the lender to speed up the payment date in the event of default, making the entire principal amount due

Accrue: to increase or accumulate. Mortgage interest is said to accrue daily

Acknowledgement: a declaration made before a notary or other official certifying that the signing of a document is of a voluntary act undertaken of ones own free will

Addendum: an attachment to a purchase agreement or to escrow instructions that alters or negotiates the transaction specifics

Adjustable Rate Mortgage: Mortgage in which the rate of interest is adjusted based on a standard rate index. Most ARM's have caps on how much the interest rate may increase

Adjustment Interval: How often the loan's rate can be changed

Affidavit: a statement sworn under oath or before a notary

Affirmation: a formal declaration regarding the truthfulness of a statement

Alternative Mortgage: 7/23 and 5/25 mortgages with a one-time rate adjustment after seven years and five years respectively Also known as a hybrid mortgage or a two-step mortgage

Amendment: A change made to correct an error or to alter an agreement.

Amortization Schedule : A timetable for the gradual repayment of a mortgage loan An amortization schedule indicates the amount of each payment applied to interest and principal, and the remaining balance after each payment is made

Amortization Term: The amount of time required to amortize (repay) a mortgage loan. The amortization term is usually expressed in months. A 30-year fixed rate mortgage, for example, has an amortization term of 360 months

Annual Percentage Rate (APR): A standardized method of calculating the cost of a mortgage, stated as a yearly rate which includes such items as interest, mortgage insurance, and certain points or credit costs

Appraisal: A written report by a qualified appraiser estimating the value of the property

Appraised Value: opinion of a property's fair market value, based on an appraiser's inspection and analysis of the property

Appraiser: A person qualified by education, training, and experience to estimate the value of real property

Appreciation: An increase in the value of a property due to changes in market conditions or improvements to the property

ARM: See Adjustable Rate Mortgage

Assessed Value: The value of a property as determined by a public tax assessor for the purpose of taxation

Assignment: the transfer, in writing, of one's interest in something

Assumable: A mortgage that a buyer can assume, or take over, from the seller of the property

Assumption: the taking over of another person's financial obligation

Balloon Mortgage: A loan that has regular monthly payments, which amortize over a stated term but call for a final lump sum (balloon payment) at the end of a specified term, or maturity date such as 10 years

Basis Points: 1/100th of 1 percent If an interest rate changes 50 basis points, for example, it has move ½ of 1 percent

Binder: See title binder
Biweekly Mortgage: A mortgage that schedules payments every two weeks instead of the standard monthly payment The 26 biweekly payments are each equal to one-half of the monthly payment. The result for the borrower is a substantial reduction in interest payments because the mortgage is paid off sooner. See also prepayment plan

Bridge loan: A loan that "bridges" the gap between the purchase of a new home and the sale of the borrower's current home. The borrower's current home is used as collateral and the money is used to close on the new home before the current home is sold. Some are structured so they completely pay off the old home's first mortgage at the bridge loan's closing. Others pile the new debt on top of the old. They usually run for a term of six months

Broker: See mortgage broker

Broker Premium: A premium paid to the mortgage broker as the "middleman" in the mortgage process between the lender and the borrower

Built-ins: Cabinets, ranges, ceiling fans and other items permanently attached to the structure, and which a buyer may assume will remain with the structure

Buy down: The process of trading money for a lower mortgage rate The borrower "buys down" the interest rate on a mortgage by paying discount points up front. It can also be a mortgage in which an initial lump sum payment is made to reduce a borrower's monthly payments during the first few years of a mortgage

Caps: The maximum amount the interest rate can change annually or cumulatively over the life of an adjustable rate mortgage. F or example, if the caps are 2 percent annual and 6 percent life of loan, a mortgage with a first-year rate of 10 percent could rise to no more than 12 percent the second year, and no more than 16 percent over the entire life of the loan

Certificate of Title: A statement provided by the Title Company or attorney stating that the title to the real estate is legally held by the current owner

Chattel: Personal property

Clear title: A title that is free of liens or legal questions as to ownership of a piece of property

Close of Escrow: the date when the documents are recorded and title passes from the seller to the buyer

Closing: The meeting at which the sale of a property is finalized The buyer signs the lender agreement for the mortgage and pays' closing costs and escrow amounts. The buyer and seller sign documents to transfer the ownership of the property. Also known as the settlement

Closing costs: Expenses incurred by buyers and sellers in transferring ownership of a property. Closing costs normally include an origination fee, an attorney's fee, taxes, escrow payments, and charges for title insurance. Lenders or Real Estate Agents provide estimates of closing costs to prospective homebuyers

Closing Statement: A financial disclosure accounting for all funds changing hands at the closing See also HUD-1 Statement

Cloud on title: Any fact or condition that could adversely affect the title

Commission: In real estate, the broker, or mortgage associates fee for assisting in the transaction Usually expressed as a percentage of the total paid by the buyer

Commitment: A formal offer by a lender stating the approved terms for lending money to a homebuyer

Common Area Assessment: A levy against individual unit owners in a condominium or planned unit development to pay for upkeep, repairs, and improvements to the property's common areas, such as corridors, elevators, parking lots, swimming pools and tennis courts

Comparables: Refers to "comparable properties" which are used for comparative purposes in the appraisal process. Comps are recently sold properties that are similar in size, location, and amenities to the home for sale. Comps help an appraiser determine the fair market value of a property

Concurrent Escrow: a procedure where the one closing is dependent on the completion of another closing. Also termed a double escrow

Condominium: A real estate project in which each unit owner has title to a unit of the project, and sometimes and undivided interest in the common areas

Conforming Loan: A loan that conforms to the standard rules for purchase by Freddie Mac or Fannie Mae

Contingency: A condition that must be met before a contract is legally binding. For example, homebuyers often include a contingency that specifies that the contract is not binding until after a satisfactory report from a home inspector

Contract: In real estate parlance, the contract is the legal document by which buyer and seller make offers and counteroffers. The real estate contract describes the property, includes or excludes items in the property, names the price, apportions the closing costs between the parties and sets forth a closing date.

When a buyer and seller agree on the terms and sign the same document the property is said to be "under contract". More formally known as the agreement for the sale, purchase agreement, or earnest money contract

Conventional Mortgage: Usually refers to a fixed-rate, 30-year mortgage that is not insured by FHA, Farmers Home Administration, or Veterans Administration

Convertible Mortgage: An adjustable rate mortgage ARM that can be converted to a fixed mortgage under specific conditions

Cooperative: A type of multiple ownership in which the residents of a multiunit housing complex own shares in the cooperative corporation that owns the property, giving each resident the right to occupy a specific apartment or unit

Cost-of-funds: A yield index based upon the cost of funds to savings & loan institution in the San Francisco Federal Home Loan Bank District. It is one of the indexes commonly used to set the rate of adjustable rate mortgages

Covenant: A written restriction on the use of land, most commonly in use today in homeowners associations

Credit report: A report on a person's credit history prepared by a credit bureau and used by a lender in determining a loan applicant's record for paying debts in a timely manner

Debt-to-Income Ratio: The percentage of a person's monthly earnings used to pay off all debt obligations Lenders consider two ratios, constructed in slightly different ways. The first called the front-end ratio, the ratio of the monthly housing expenses – including principal, interest, property taxes, and insurance, (PITI) is compared to the borrower's gross, pretax monthly income. In the back-end ratio, a borrower's other debts such as auto loans and credit cards are figured in. Lenders usually consider both and set an acceptable ratio. Some lenders and some lending qualifying agencies only consider the back-end ratio

Deed: The legal document conveying title to the property

Depreciation: A decline in the value of a property as opposed to appreciation

Disbursement: the release of funds held in an escrow account

Discount Points: A type of point (1 percent of the loan) paid by the borrower to reduce the interest rate

Down payment: The amount of a property's purchase price that the buyer pays in cash and does not finance with a mortgage

Earnest money: A deposit made by potential homebuyers during negotiations with the seller. The sum shows a seller that the buyer is serious about purchasing a property

80-10-10 Loan: A combination of an 80 percent loan-to-value first mortgage, a 10 percent down payment and a 10 percent home equity loan. This is also sometimes referred to as a CLTV (Combined Loan-to-Value)

Encumbrance: A lien, charge or liability against a property

Endorsement: an addition that either expands or limits the standard coverage's provided under a title insurance policy

Equal Credit: A federal law that requires lenders and other creditors to make credit equally available with out discrimination based on race, color, religion, national origin, age, sex, marital status, or receipt of income from public assistance programs

Equity: The value of a homeowner's unencumbered interest in real estate Equity is the difference between the homes fair market value and the unpaid balance of the mortgage and any outstanding liens Equity increases as the mortgage is paid down or as the property enjoys appreciation

Escrow Payment: The portion of a homeowner's monthly mortgage payment that is held by the loan servicer to pay for taxes and insurance Also known as reserves The loan servicer holds the escrow funds separately from money meant to pay principal and interest

Fair Credit Reporting Act: A consumer protection law that regulates the disclosure of consumer credit reports

by credit reporting agencies and establishes procedures for correcting mistakes on a person's credit record

Fannie Mae: Nickname for Federal National Mortgage Association It is a government-chartered non-bank financial services company and the nation's largest source of financing for home mortgages It was started to make sure mortgage money is available in all areas of the country

FHA Mortgage: A mortgage insured by the Federal Housing Administration

First mortgage: A mortgage that is the primary lien against a property

Fixed-rate Mortgage: A mortgage in which the interest rate does not change during the entire term of the loan, most often 15 or 30 years

Flood Insurance Insurance that compensates for the physical property damage resulting from rising water It is required for properties located in federally designated flood areas

Foreclosure: The legal process by which a homeowner in default on a mortgage is deprived of interest in the property This usually involves a forced sale of the property at public auction with the proceeds of the sale being applied to the mortgage debt

Freddie Mac: Nickname for Federal Home Loan Mortgage Corp A financial corporation chartered by the federal government to buy pools of mortgages from lenders and sell securities backed by these mortgages

Ginnie Mae: Nickname for the Government National Mortgage Association

Good Faith Estimate: A written estimate of closing costs that the lender must provide to prospective homebuyers within three days of submitting a mortgage loan application

Government National Mortgage Association (Ginnie Mae) A government-owned corporation within the US Department of Housing and Urban Development (HUD) Created by Congress in 1968, GNMA has responsibility for the special assistance loan program known as Ginnie Mae

Hazard Insurance: Insurance coverage that compensates for physical damage to property from natural disasters such as fire and other hazards Depending on where a piece of property is located, lenders may also require flood insurance or policies covering windstorms (hurricanes) or earthquakes

Home Inspection: An inspection by a building professional that evaluates the structural and mechanical condition of a property

Homeowners Association: A nonprofit association that manages the common areas of a condominium or PUD Unit owners pay the association a fee to maintain areas owned jointly

Homeowner's Insurance: An insurance policy that combines personal liability insurance and hazard insurance coverage for a residence and its contents

Housing Expense: The percentage of gross monthly income that goes toward paying a Ratio mortgage or rent on a home

HUD-1: The document with an itemized listing of closing costs payable at the closing or settlement meeting when buying property The closing costs can include a commission, loan fees, and points, and sums set aside for escrow payments, taxes, and insurance It is signed by both the buyer and the seller, who may be paying some of the closing costs The statement form is published by HUD

Hybrid Mortgage: See alternative mortgage products.

Index: A published measure of the cost of money that lenders use to calculate the rate on an ARM The most common indexes are the one-year Treasury Constant Maturity Yield and the FHLB 11th District Cost of Funds

Indexed Rate: The sum of the published index plus the margin For example, if the index were 9 percent and the margin 2.75 percent, the indexed rate would be 11.75 percent. Often, lenders charge less than the indexed rate the first year of an ARM

Initial Interest Rate: Starting rate of an ARM

Interest Tax Deduction: Most mortgage holders can deduct all the interest paid on the loan in filing income tax The deduction applies to people with just on mortgage on a primary residence, as well

as those with a combination of loans. Within certain time limits set by the IRS, points paid up front on a mortgage are usually deductible in the year the house was purchased

Jumbo Mortgage: Mortgages larger than the limits set by Fannie Mae and Freddie Mac. A jumbo mortgage will carry a higher interest rate than a conventional mortgage

Lease-purchase   A financing option that allows a potential homebuyer to lease a property with the option to buy   Often constructed so the monthly rent payment covers the owner's first mortgage payment, plus an additional amount as a savings deposit to accumulate cash for a down payment   A seller may agree to a lease-purchase option if the housing market is saturated and the seller is having a difficult time selling the property

Lien: A legal hold or claim from one person on the property of another   The lien placed by a first mortgage is special. It is called a first lien and takes precedence over others

Lifetime Rate Cap: In an ARM, it limits the amount that the interest rate can increase or decrease over the life of the loan. See also caps

Lis Pendens: A pending lawsuit; in real estate, the constructive notice filed in public records that a legal dispute exists over a piece of property

Livery of Seizen: Under common law, the process of transferring title

Loan Origination: The process by which a mortgage lender obtains a mortgage secured by real property An origination fee is charged by the lender to process all forms involved in obtaining a mortgage

Loan-to-value (LTV) Ratio: The ratio of a mortgage loan amount to the property's appraised value or selling price, whichever is less For example, if a home is sold for $100,000 and the mortgage amount is $80,000 the LTV is 80%

Lock: Lender's guarantee that the mortgage rate quoted will be good for a specific amount of time. The homebuyer usually wants the lock to stay in effect until the date of the closing

Lock-and-Float: Rate programs offered by companies that allow borrowers to lock in the current interest rate on a mortgage for a specified period, while also letting them "float" the rate down if market conditions improve before closing

Low-down Mortgages: Mortgages with a low down payment, usually less than 10 percent. Frannie Mae and Freddie Mac design loan programs that spell out a set of standards for lenders. In recent years, these government-chartered agencies have made low-down mortgages more available

Margin: The number of percentage points added to the index on a one-year ARM

Maturity: The date on which the principal balance of a loan becomes due and payable

Mortgage: A legal document that uses property as collateral to secure payment of a debt

Mortgage Banker: The lender that originates a mortgage loan, the one making the loan directly and closing the loan

Mortgage Broker: An individual or company that brings borrowers and lenders together for the purpose of loan origination Unlike a mortgage banker, brokers do not fund the loan but work on behalf of several lenders. Brokers typically require a fee or a commission for their service See broker premium

Mortgage Insurance: A policy that insures the lender against loss should the homeowner default on a mortgage. Depending on the loan, the insurance can be issued by government agencies such as the FHA or a private company. It is part of the monthly mortgage payment. (See also private mortgage insurance PMI)

Negative Amortization: A gradual increase in mortgage debt that happens when a monthly payment does not cover the entire principal and interest due The shortfall is added to the remaining balance to create "negative" amortization

No-doc or low-doc Loan: These no-documentation or low-documentation loans are designed for the entrepreneur or self-employed, for recent immigrants with money in foreign countries or for borrowers who cannot or choose not to reveal information about their incomes

Note: The document giving evidence of mortgage indebtedness, including the amount and terms of repayment

Origination Fee: A fee paid to the lender for processing a loan application

Owner financing A transaction in which the seller of a house provides all or part of the financing Sellers may provide financing because they need to sell the property right away or they are having difficulty selling the house and want to provide financing as an incentive to a buyer

Periodic rate cap: In an ARM, it limits how much an interest rate can increase or decrease during any one-adjustment period See also caps

PITI: Stands for principal, interest, taxes and insurance that are the usual components of a monthly mortgage payment

PITI Reserves: A cash amount that a homebuyer must have on hand after making a down payment and paying all closing costs The reserves required by a lender must equal the amount a buyer would pay for PITI for a specific number of months

Plat: A map that shows a parcel of land and how it is subdivided into individual lots Plat maps also show the locations of streets and easements

PMI: See private mortgage insurance

Points: A point equals 1 percent of a mortgage loan. Lenders charge points as a way to make a profit. Borrowers may pay discount points to reduce the loan interest rate. Buyers are prohibited from paying points on HUD or VA guaranteed loans

Pre-approval: This process goes a step further than pre-qualification. It means the lender has contacted the borrower's employer, bank, and other places to verify all claims of earnings and assets. In return, the borrower receives a letter stating the lender is willing to grant a mortgage for a specific amount within a limited period with the stipulation that there are no material changes to the borrower's situation

Prepayment Penalty: A fee imposed by certain lenders if the first mortgage is paid off early

Prepayment Plan: Similar to biweekly mortgage, but operated by a third party   In it, the borrower pays to the third party, half the monthly mortgage payment every two weeks At the end of the year, the plan operators typically take the extra money that results from the process and sends lump sum payment to the participants' lenders

Pre-qualification: An early evaluation by a lender of a potential homebuyer's credit report, plus earnings, savings, and debt information   The homebuyer gets a non-binding estimate of the mortgage amount the borrower would qualify for, or how much house the borrower can afford. Buyers who pre-qualify can go a step further and seek a pre-approval

Rate Lock: A commitment issued by a lender to the homebuyer or the mortgage broker guaranteeing a specific interest rate for a specified amount of time See also lock

Real Estate Agent: A person licensed to negotiate and transact the sale of real estate on behalf of the property owner

RESPA: Real Estate Settlement Procedures Act A consumer protection law that requires lenders to give homebuyers advance notice of closing costs, which are payable at the closing or settlement meeting

Realtor: A real estate broker or an associate who holds an active membership in a local real estate board that is affiliated with the National Association of Realtors

Refinancing: Securing a new loan in order to pay off the existing mortgage or to gain access to the existing equity in the home

Roll-in Loan: A refinance loan that rolls any closing costs or fees into the loan. These programs best serve people who have a reasonable amount of equity, want to reduce their overall interest expense, and plan to stay in their homes

Rural Housing Service (RHS): The agency in the US Department of Agriculture providing financing to farmers and other qualified borrowers buying property in rural areas who are unable to obtain loans elsewhere. It offers low-interest-rate loans with no down payment to borrowers with low-to-moderate incomes who live in rural areas or small towns

Sales Agreement: A written contract signed by the buyer and the seller of a house stating the terms and conditions under which the property will be sold

Second Mortgage: A mortgage on the property that has a lien position behind the first mortgage

Servicer: An organization that collects monthly mortgage principal and interest payments from homeowners and manages escrow accounts for paying taxes and homeowners' insurance premiums The servicer often services mortgages that have been purchased by an investor in the secondary mortgage market

Settlement: See closing

Sub-prime Mortgage: A mortgage granted to a borrower considered sub-prime, that is, a person with a less-than perfect credit report. Sub-prime borrowers either have missed payments on a debt or have been late with payments. Lenders charge a higher interest rate to compensate for potential losses from customers who may run into trouble and default

Time is of the Essence: A phrase inserted in contracts to require a punctual performance

Title: A legal document proving a person's right to claim entitlement to a property, including the history of the property's ownership

Title Binder: Written evidence of temporary title insurance coverage

Title Company: A company that specializes in examining and insuring titles to real estate

Title insurance: Insurance that protects against loss from disputes over ownership of a property. A policy may protect the mortgage lender and/or the homebuyer

Title search: A check of title records to ensure that the seller is the legal owner of a property and that there are no liens or other claims against the property

Transfer Tax: State or local tax levied when title passes from one owner to another

Treasury Index: An index used to determine interest rate changes for certain ARM mortgages. It is based on the results of auctions that the US Treasury holds for its Treasury bills and securities or is derived from the US Treasury's daily yield curve, which is based on the closing market bid yields on actively traded Treasury securities in the over-the-counter market

Truth-in-Lending Act (TILA): A federal law that requires lenders to disclose, in writing, the terms and conditions of a mortgage, including the annual percentage rate APR and other charges

Underwriter   A company or person undertaking the responsibility for issuing a mortgage Underwriters analyze a borrower's credit worthiness and set the loan amount

VA Mortgage: A loan backed by the Veterans Administration. It requires very low or no down payments and has less stringent requirements for qualification. Members of the US armed forces are eligible for the loans under certain qualifying conditions

Wraparound Mortgage: A new mortgage that includes the remaining balance on the old mortgage plus a new amount

Note Broker

Expanded Guide

Note Brokering Self-Study Workbook

1. _____ What transactions generated the popularity of note brokering?

_____

_____

_____

2. _____ Why would a business be interested in working with you?

_____

_____

_____

3. _____ Why would a home seller be interested in your services?

_____

_____

_____

4. _____ Why are your services valuable to a note holder?

_____

_____

_____

5. _____ Why are your services valuable to a note investor?

_____

_____

_____

6. _____ What functions beyond just bringing individuals together must you perform?

_____

_____

_____

7. _____ Explain the integral factor of note brokering.

_____

_____

_____

8. Name four of the most common notes you will encounter.

_____

_____

_____

9. What basic factors effect note desirability to an investor?

_____

_____

_____

10. What are the primary reasons mortgage notes are commonplace in every region of the country?

_____

_____

_____

11. How is a first mortgage note created?

_____

_____

_____

12. What functions will the seller typically perform for you in a 1st mortgage transaction?

_____

_____

_____

13. Why are mortgage notes attractive to note investors?

_____

_____

_____

14 What are the two most common reasons a 2nd mortgage note will exist?

_____

_____

_____

15   Why is the appraisal of high importance in a 2nd mortgage transaction?

16   Why will borrower credibility be more closely scrutinized in a 2nd mortgage transaction?

17   How is a business finance note different from a personal finance note?

18   What documentation might be used for proof of borrower capital investment in a business finance note?

19   Why are business net billing notes an excellent investment for the note investor?

20   Why are structured settlement purchases a secure investment for the note investor?

21   What three common factors must all brokered notes contained?

22   What is an income stream?

_____

_____

_____

23   What are the two most common methods of income generations from a note?

_____

_____

_____

24   What is the purpose of charging interest on a note?

_____

_____

_____

25   What income will a note investor factor when considering a purchase?

_____

_____

_____

26   What should you remember with regard to a note investor and security?

_____

_____

_____

38   What does an appraisal tell the note investor?

_____

_____

_____

39   What is another term for seller finance?

_____

_____

_____

40   Name three reasons a seller may choose to hold a note on their property.

_____

_____

_____

41   How does holding a note assist the seller in sourcing more buyers for their property?

_____

_____

_____

42   How does holding the note assist the seller in gaining more funds from the sale of the property?

_____

_____

_____

43   What advanced tactic does understanding the initial benefits of a seller held note have for you?

_____

_____

_____

44   Explain the opportunity generated for the note holder to work with you when they hold a creative finance.

_____

_____

_____

45   What is the fundamental reason for investing?

_____

_____

_____

46   What three items contribute to the note profitability?

_____

_____

_____

47   The note discount process is similar to what action in conventional marketplace finance?

_____

_____

_____

48   How does an equity position in a note investment benefit the note investor?

_____

_____

_____

49   How does the early payoff of a note through refinance or other methods affect the note investor's expected return?

_____

_____

_____

50   What is the potential investment return if the buyer pays the note as agreed, over the full note term and the investor lends $102,000 at 6.5% over 30 years?

_____

_____

_____

51   When factoring total interest income expected from a mortgage note what should you consider?

_____

_____

_____

52   What security and transaction specific documents can you expect the note investor to request?

_____

_____

_____

53   What credit based documents will the note investor typically request?

_____

_____

_____

54   What are your responsibilities with regard to package documentation?

_____

_____

_____

55   What benefit does a properly documented loan package provide the investor?

_____

_____

_____

56   Why is the note investor interested in the income of the individuals making payments on the note?

_____

_____

_____

57   Who is actually lending money in a seller held transaction?

_____

_____

_____

_____

58   What is meant by potential value?

_____

_____

_____

59   What is a promissory note?

_____

_____

_____

60   What components must be present in the note?

_____

_____

_____

62   What common information could be present on the note?

_____

_____

_____

63   What is the function of a mortgage?

_____

_____

_____

64   How is a mortgage different from a note?

_____

_____

_____

65   What does the settlement statement tell the note investor?

_____

_____

_____

66   What benefit does collateral provide the investor?

_____

_____

_____

67   What will comparison between the amortization schedule from the original transaction and the transaction detail specific amortization schedule show the investor?

_____

_____

_____

68   Why is the mortgage history important in the note assessment?

_____

_____

_____

69   What stability information will the note investor wish to review in their assessment process?

_____

_____

_____

70   What is your most important product?

_____

_____

_____

71   Why do you keep a copy of any query that does not lead to a full package?

_____

_____

_____

72   Why do you ask for the note specifics such as note rate and note term at the time of the initial interview?

_____

_____

_____

73   Why is it important to determine the age or 1st payment date of the note at the time of the initial interview?

_____

_____

_____

74   What does a credit report show about a borrower?

_____

_____

_____

75   What is your primary concern when reviewing a borrower's credit report?

_____

_____

_____

76   What is the score range you can expect to see on a credit report?

_____

_____

_____

77   What are the three credit bureaus you will encounter?

_____

_____

_____

78   What is a FICO?

_____

_____

_____

79   How is the FICO generated?

_____

_____

_____

80   What do credit bureau scores provide to an investor?

_____

_____

_____

81   How can you gain information to assist you in understanding why a credit report scored the way it did?

_____

_____

_____

82   What is a compensating factor?

_____

_____

_____

83   Why do you use compensating factors?

_____

_____

84   Name three potential compensating factors:

_____

_____

85   What does a debt ratio tell you about a file?

_____

_____

86   Name three items not commonly factored into the debt ratio:

_____

_____

98   How many times do you factor each debt when calculating debt ratios?

_____

_____

99   Why is an appraisal vital to the note process?

_____

_____

100   What is a red flag?

_____

_____

101   What is URAR?

_____

_____

_____

102   What is your goal when reviewing an appraisal?

_____

_____

_____

103   What action should you take if you discover an error in a loan document?

_____

_____

_____

104   Why is it important to locate red flags early in the process?

_____

_____

_____

105   What alterations should you make to a completed appraisal if you discover an issue during your review?

_____

_____

_____

106   What does the sales comparison valuation approach consider?

_____

_____

_____

107   Why is it beneficial to use reference numbers for submissions rather than contact information?

_____

_____

_____

108   What is the face value of a note?

_____

_____

_____

109   Name two reasons you should include the monthly payment figure in the submission.

_____

_____

_____

110   Why would a note contain a balloon payment requirement?

_____

_____

_____

111   Explain why low DTI Ratio are desirable to an investor.

_____

_____

_____

112   What is the first reason an investor will require the note to be discounted?

_____

_____

_____

113   What is meant by futures?

_____

_____

_____

114   What is the second reason a note will be discounted at the time of purchase?

_____

_____

_____

115   How will your commission or payment be generated in the discount process?

_____

_____

_____

116   What other method may you employ other than the discount to generate income?

_____

_____

_____

117   What are three activities you will perform in the note process?

_____

_____

_____

118   What is the finder's fee?

_____

_____

_____

119   Why would it benefit you to accept the finder's fee on a transaction and turn the remaining negotiations over to the investor thereby losing any possible discount commission?

_____

_____

_____

120   When would a flat fee commission from the seller be paid?

_____

_____

_____

121   How do you determine what commission and activity structure you prefer to employ in the brokering process?

_____

_____

_____

_____

122   What occurs when an investor is willing to pay a higher premium for a note the seller has agreed to accept?

_____

_____

_____

123   What three common payment methods are available to you as the note broker?

_____

_____

_____

124   Why is it important to have a solid relationship with your closing attorney or settlement company?

_____

_____

_____

125   Why is it desirable to have the transaction funds to the settlement company prior to the date of closing rather than having the note investor bring a check to settlement?

_____

_____

_____

126   When will you typically receive your commission check from the settlement agent?

_____

_____

_____

127   Why would you wish to perform additional services for your investor or note holder?

_____

_____

_____

128   Name three activities that may occur following the settlement meeting.

_____

_____

_____

129   Why is it important to notify the hazard insurance company of the transaction?

_____

_____

_____

130   Why may you find it beneficial to focus on fewer note types early in your career?

_____

_____

_____

131   What screening factors may assist you in choosing investor partners?

_____

_____

_____

_____

132   What is it vital to remember with regard to your image?

_____

_____

_____

_____

133   How will the abundance of time available for marketing assist you in solidifying your career?

_____

_____

_____

135   How will the referral data on a pre-qualification questionnaire benefit your marketing plan?

_____

_____

_____

_____

136   What are the most common marketing options available to the note broker?

_____

_____

_____

_____

137   Name the first two marketing methods you should employ as a beginning note broker.

_____

_____

_____

1.   The popularity of note brokering has grown in tandem with
       a.   higher mortgage rates
       b.   seller finance transactions
       c.   accelerated sub-prime base
       d.   none of the above

2.   Businesses provide revolving credit terms to buyers of
       a.   30 days
       b.   60 days
       c.   90 days
       d.   any of the above

3.   Note brokering provides the note holder with
       a.   an excellent investment opportunity
       b.   periodic payments
       c.   a lump sum of cash
       d.   none of the above

4.   As a note broker you will be working for
       a.   the note holder
       b.   the note investor
       c.   personal gain
       d.   all of the above

5.   Fulfilling every promise will
       a.   generate referrals
       b.   ensure repeat business
       c.   grow your business
       d.   all of the above

6.   You should structure your business around the premise that all parties to the transaction should walk away
       satisfied that they received the best possible deal.
       a.   True
       b.   False

7.   It is your purpose to act as a
        a.   liaison between the note holder and note investor
        b.   educator in the note brokering process
        c.   negotiation advocate for each party
        d.   all of the above

8.   The most common note you will encounter will be
        a.   1st mortgage notes
        b.   unsecured notes
        c.   revolving notes
        d.   any of the above

9   What situation creates a note?
        a.   Any situation where an individual receives a lump sum
        b.   Any situation where an individual receives a period payment
        c.   Any situation in which the exchange of funds occur
        d.   None of the above

10   What item may make up a note payment?
        a.   principal and interest
        b.   penalties
        c.   finance charges
        d.   any of the above

11   A first mortgage note will contain
        a.   unsecured property
        b.   personal property
        c.   real property
        d.   any of the above

12   The security level of a mortgage note investment is
        a.   high
        b.   low
        c.   reasonable risk
        d.   none of the above

13   Second mortgage notes often occur
        a.   rarely
        b.   as a result of lender requirements
        c.   when a seller requires an additional return
        d.   any of the above

14   An appraisal is a critical element in a 2nd mortgage transaction
        a.   True
        b.   False

15   A business note will not contain real property as part of the transaction.
        a.   True
        b.   False

16   An investor may sometimes request a copy of the borrower's resume before making a note investment decision.

        a.   True
        b.   False

17 A business invoice is a(n)
   a.   excellent return for the investor
   b.   faster return on investment than some other notes
   c.   potentially recurring transaction
   d.   any of the above

18. Insurance or structured settlements are often
   a.   riskier than other note investments
   b.   court ordered making the investment less risky
   c.   structured to make note investment difficult
   d.   any of the above

19 A saleable note must contain
   a.   an anxious seller
   b.   a pre-set discount agreement
   c.   an income stream
   d.   all of the above

20 An income stream is
   a.   constantly flowing funding
   b.   periodic payments against a lump sum
   c.   a note investors portfolio
   d.   none of the above

21 Interest payments compensate the note holder for
   a.   the transaction workload
   b.   the time they will wait for a return
   c.   the discounted value of the note
   d.   all of the above

22 A note is as valuable as it's ability to
   a.   be sold to an investor.
   b.   generate a positive cash flow
   c.   secure against real property
   d.   all of the above

23 Most note investors are interested in obtaining the collateral of a note.
   a.   True
   b.   False

24 An appraisal will help the investor determine the
   a.   condition of the property
   b.   condition of the neighborhood
   c.   value of the property
   d.   all of the above

25 A note investor protects their interest by assessing
   a.   transaction details
   b.   borrower profile
   c.   property profile
   d.   all of the above

26   It is usually possible to predict a borrower's performance with 100% accuracy when the proper documentation is obtained.
    a.   True
    b.   False

27   Note holders will frequently create the note because
    a.   they desire a higher return on investment
    b.   the buyer is unable to provide the desired funds at purchase
    c.   the buyer is willing to pay a higher interest rate
    d.   all of the above

28   A seller-financed transaction might enable the seller to
    a.   sell faster
    b.   obtain more money
    c.   earn extra income
    d.   all of the above

29   Creative finance allows the seller to
    a.   receive periodic payments
    b.   earn interest like the bank
    c.   become a lender
    d.   all of the above

30   Most note holders will prefer a lump sum of cash to periodic payments despite the enhanced income potential to be gained with the periodic payments.
    a.   True
    b.   False

31   Most note transactions provide two methods of obtaining a return on investment to the note investor.
    a.   True
    b.   False

32   In a note brokering transaction
    a.   the seller must walk away satisfied with the transaction
    b.   the investor must walk away satisfied with the transaction
    c.   you must walk away satisfied with the transaction
    d.   everyone should walk away satisfied with the transaction

33   Which of the following is not a method of earning a return on investment capital?
    a.   finance charges
    b.   discount negotiation
    c.   location
    d.   none of the above

34   Risk is not a factor to consider when choosing to purchase a note.
    a.   True
    b.   False

35   A consideration a note investor might wish the note holder to think about is
    a.   the buyer's risk assessment level
    b.   the current face value of a note
    c.   the items a seller might use the cash out funds to purchase
    d.   all of the above

36   An investor who buys notes desires an equity position.
      a.   True
      b.   False

37   What figure is used as the basis figure upon which the discount will apply?
      a.   The face value of the note
      b.   The appraised value of the property
      c.   The original note amount
      d.   None of the above

38   The potential risk is one factor in the discounted offer an investor might make on a note.
      a.   True
      b.   False

39   One benefit to a note holder when selling a note is
      a.   the receipt of the full face value of the note
      b.   a more stable monthly payment
      c.   the ability to use the lump sum payment immediately
      d.   all of the above

480   The cash out amount is the face value of the note.
      a.   True
      b.   False

41   The greatest potential profit in a note is usually generated from
      a.   interest
      b.   equity
      c.   principal
      d.   none of the above

42   The first payments on a mortgage note typically go toward interest.
      a.   True
      b.   False

43   A potential consideration when assessing a note is the security shown by
      a.   payment history
      b.   appraisal assessment
      c.   terms of the transaction
      d.   all of the above

44   Amortization schedules assist in gaining an overview of the transaction.
      a.   True
      b.   False

45   The main function of the appraisal of the property is to determine the
      a.   note amount
      b.   property market value
      c.   hazard insurance type
      d.   all of the above

50   An appraisal might show if a property has outdated services such as electrical.
- a.   True
- b.   False

51   A factor pertaining to the individual making payments on the note that might be considered when assessing creditworthiness of an individual making payments on a note is
- a.   explanation of derogatory credit information
- b.   income and debt structure
- c.   payment history on the note
- d.   all of the above

52   If an individual making payments on the note has had many different jobs over the previous two years the note investor will not be concerned as long as there are no long gaps in employment.
- a.   True
- b.   False

53   What is the best source of proof that mortgage payments have been made in a timely manner if there is no inclusion regarding the account on the credit report?
- a.   A letter from the mortgage holder stating payment status
- b.   A verbal confirmation from the mortgage holder of account status
- c.   Cancelled checks from each month of the payment term
- d.   Any of the above

54   Having a large pool of potential investors is more important than documenting a loan package to meet the guidelines of particular investors.
- a.   True
- b.   False

55   Which factor might cause concern when reviewing the history of the individual making payments on a note?
- a.   A delay in payment on many accounts due to a provable injury
- b.   The utilities are frequently disconnected due to non-payment
- c.   Mortgage payments that are typically 30-45 days late but always paid
- d.   All of the above

56.   Note Investors review many note packages so it is best to provide as little documentation as necessary to minimize their time investment and strengthen relationships.
- a.   True
- b.   False

57   The note holder will often be involved in
- a.   negotiating the interest rate
- b.   setting up a payment plan
- c.   qualifying the borrower
- d.   all of the above

58   The interest rate charged on a seller financed note is typically based upon the average rate charged by conventional lending institutions.
- a.   True
- b.   False

59   To be legally binding a note would require
- a.   a verbal agreement
- b.   the terms of the transaction
- c.   the signature of the note investor
- d.   all of the above

60   A promissory note does not require
- a.   the interest rate be detailed
- b.   the late payment stipulations to be detailed
- c.   the appraised value to be included
- d.   none of the above

61   A promissory note is designed to protect the seller.
- a.   True
- b.   False

62   A mortgagor is the property against which a note is secured.
- a.   True
- b.   False

63   A lender may enforce the full payment requirement of the note under the acceleration clause if the real estate property taxes are not paid.
- a.   True
- b.   False

64   If the property is sold to another individual the loan balance can typically be called due and payable if
- a.   the convenant of preservation is included
- b.   if the alienation clause is included
- c.   if the satisfaction of mortgage document is created
- d.   none of the above

65   The pre-approval questionnaire contains
- a.   all of the information you will need from the borrower
- b.   most of the information you will need for the initial submittal
- c.   all of the information the investor team will require
- d.   most of the information necessary to close the loan

66   The initial contact
- a.   sets the tone for your relationship with the client
- b.   is the most essential information gathering period
- c.   sets the note program you will use for the package
- d.   none of the above

67   You will request a credit authorization verbally before pulling borrower credit.
- a.   True
- b.   False

68   You may enter common nicknames for the borrower
- a.   True
- b.   False

69.   You must always have a co-borrower for the loan
- a.   True
- b.   False

70   Your most important product is
      a.   low discount requirements
      b.   professionalism and responsiveness
      c.   simple remittal procedures
      d.   none of the above

71   The pre-qualification questionnaire will provide you with
      a.   answers to every question on the questionnaire
      b.   information that will be noted in the explanation of credit section
      c.   all of the required documentation
      d.   none of the above

72   Credit Reports are:
      A.   A great way to see how many things people buy
      B.   A way to get to know a borrower's likes and dislikes
      C.   An overview of a person's entire history of spending and payment
      D.   None of the above

73   Credit reports are an overview of a person's entire history of spending and payment habits.
      A.   True
      B.   False

74   The ability to borrow more money is affected by
      A.   How much debt potential a borrower currently carries
      B.   How many things a borrower has in his house
      C.   How a borrower treats you and your company
      D.   All of the above

75   A bankruptcy can remain on a credit report for
      A.   3 years
      B.   7 years
      C.   10 years
      D.   Life

76   Accounts to medical services that a borrower has failed to pay as agreed are
      A.   Often treated differently
      B.   Never a concern
      C.   An underwriting condition
      D.   Always to be paid in full

77   Repeatedly requesting a borrower's credit report may
      A.   Adversely effect the credit score
      B.   Show the borrower's can obtain further credit
      C.   Cause an investor condition
      D.   All of the above

78   Debt to Income is
      A.   The amount of debt a borrower carries
      B.   The amount of income a borrower brings home
      C.   The amount of income a borrower makes before taxes
      D.   None of the above

79   A late payment is any payment paid past the due date even when within the grace period
      A.   True
      B.   False

80   Credit bureau scores are based upon
      A.   Every action taken by a borrower with regard to debt
      B.   The data contained within the credit bureau
      C.   All information contained within the loan application
      D.   None of the above

81   A credit bureau score will rank order potential borrowers based upon the number of good loans to bad loans.
      A.   True
      B.   False

82   The property in a loan process is as important a factor as borrower history
      A. True
      B. False

83   The appraisal will be used for
      A. Equity assessment
      B. Title insurance
      C. LTV Assessment
      D. All of the above

81   URAR is an abbreviation for
      A. The Uniform Residential Appraisal Report
      B. The 1004
      C. The most common appraisal you will encounter
      D. All of the above

85   The appraiser will note Red Flags during the appraisal process
      A. True
      B. False

86   The appraiser will assess
      A. The property
      B. The neighborhood
      C. Recently sold property
      D. All of the above

87   You should never read the appraisal before submitting it to the investor
      A. True
      B. False

88   If you note a discrepancy, error or issue on the appraisal report you should
      A. Notify the investor
      B. Influence the appraiser to alter the item
      C. Notify the appraiser of the issue
      D. Request a different appraisal

89   Property Valuation will be determined by
       A. Comparison with other property
       B. Sales price of other property
       C. Proximity to recently sold property
       D. All of the above

90   You should provide the parties with reference numbers rather than names early in the process to
       a.   ensure your commission
       b.   protect the privacy between parties
       c.   allow the note investor to remain anonymous
       d.   all of the above

91   Placing your contact information on the submission sheet
       a.   ensures you will receive a response
       b.   saves the note investor time
       c.   allows you to remain in the note process
       d.   none of the above

92   The face value of the note is
       a.   the originally negotiated sales price
       b.   total principal figure due at submission
       c.   total of principal and interest the investor will receive
       d.   none of the above

93   Seasoning is
       a.   the length of time the investor will collect on a note
       b.   the length of time the note has been in existence
       c.   the length of time the seller has owned the note-generating instrument
       d.   none of the above

94   A balloon payment is a
       a.   larger than normal payment
       b.   amount the seller will receive at settlement
       c.   lump sum amount received on the transaction
       d.   none of the above

95.   Payments are always fixed at 12 per year.
       a.   True
       b.   False

96   All note investors will use credit scores as part of their note analysis.
       a.   True
       b.   False

97   Payment history allows the investor to
       a.   calculate discounts
       b.   predict the future payments
       c.   negotiate with the seller
       d.   all of the above

98   The higher the DTI Ratio the
- a.   higher the monthly cash flow
- b.   lower the monthly cash flow
- c.   higher the chance the buyer will perform as agreed
- d.   none of the above

99   You should remit all available documents at the time of the initial submittal.
- a.   True
- b.   False

100   Notes will be discounted in an effort to
- a.   satisfy the note seller
- b.   ensure profitability to the note broker
- c.   generate a lower monthly payment requirement
- d.   any of the above

101   The higher the equity held in an investment the
- a.   higher the risk of default
- b.   lower the risk of default
- c.   higher the commission structure
- d.   none of the above

102   It is possible for the note broker to negotiate
- a.   1 large payment in the transaction
- b.   2 different payments in the transaction
- c.   3 different payments in the transaction
- d.   any of the above

103   An finders fee may be negotiated with the
- a.   individual making payments on the note
- b.   note investor
- c.   mortgage lender
- d.   any of the above

104   After receiving the finders fee you may
- a.   accept your payment and move on to the next transaction
- b.   continue the negotiation activity in the transaction
- c.   allow the investor and seller to negotiate the remaining transaction details
- d.   all of the above

105   The note broker may actually earn more in the discount process than the note investor.
- a.   True
- b.   False

106   You will earn income by negotiating a
- a.   lower discount percentage with the investor
- b.   higher discount percentage with the seller
- c.   flat finders fee with either party
- d.   all of the above

107   A settlement meeting requires the attendance of all parties.
- a.   True
- b.   False

108   It is imperative that you create a solid relationship with your settlement company because
    a.   it will create smoother settlement meetings.
    b.   it will limit transaction issues at the meeting.
    c.   it will assist in keeping figures private.
    d.   all of the above

109   The discount commission you negotiated will be
    a.   paid out of the seller's lump sum
    b.   paid out of the investor's purchase price
    c.   a typically undisclosed figure
    d.   all of the above

110   The checks for the settlement should be
    a.   written by the note investor prior to the settlement
    b.   generated by the settlement agent during or after the settlement
    c.   exchanged at the settlement meeting
    d.   none of the above

111   All parties must remain at the settlement meeting until the transaction is complete.
    a.   True
    b.   False

112   The responsibility of a customer service oriented note broker will
    a.   end with a successful settlement meeting
    b.   continue beyond the settlement meeting
    c.   end when the parties are satisfied with the transaction
    d.   none of the above

113   Recording of transaction documents must be completed
    a.   before the note holder receives their check
    b.   before the settlement agent can release any checks
    c.   before the note investor pays any funds
    d.   none of the above

114   After settlement, you can assist the note investor by
    a.   contacting the hazard insurance company
    b.   issuing notification of servicing transfer
    c.   notify senior lien holders of the transfer
    d.   any of the above

115   Exceptional customer service in each transaction may assist you in
    a.   obtaining future referral business
    b.   expanding your business
    c.   ensuring future note investor interest
    d.   all of the above

116   As a beginning note broker, it is beneficial to experiment with each type of note available for brokering.
    a.   True
    b.   False

117   As a new note investor, it is best to work
    a.   out of your own office
    b.   out of your home office
    c.   out of an established brokerage
    d.   any of the above

118   Early in your career as a note broker you will have
    a.   ample referrals to begin growing your business
    b.   limited marketing time available to you
    c.   ample time to experiment with marketing techniques
    d.   none of the above

119   It is best to follow the proven marketing plan used by all other note brokers.
    a.   True
    b.   False

120   Print advertisements will typically provide you with
    a.   the ability to convey information
    b.   name recognition
    c.   media saturation
    d.   all of the above

www.ingramcontent.com/pod-product-compliance
Lightning Source LLC
Chambersburg PA
CBHW082354270326
41935CB00013B/1618